PROGRESSIVE

Complete
Learn To Play
CLASSICAL GUITAR

Manual

by
Jason Waldron

Visit our Website
www.learntoplaymusic.com

The Progressive Series of Music Instruction Books, CDs and DVDs

2

CONTENTS

CONTENTS CONT.

CONTENTS CONT.

CONTENTS CONT.

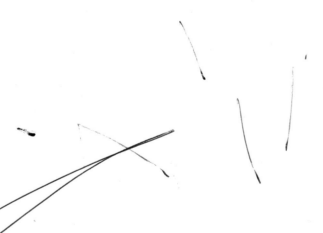

PROGRESSIVE COMPLETE LEARN TO PLAY CLASSICAL GUITAR MANUAL
I.S.B.N. 978 1 86469 239 6
Order Code: CP-69239
Acknowledgments
Cover Photograph: Phil Martin
Photographs: Phil Martin

For more information on this series contact;
LTP Publishing PTY LTD
email: info@learntoplaymusic.com
or visit our website;
www.learntoplaymusic.com

Published by
KOALA MUSIC ™
PUBLICATIONS

INTRODUCTION

Progressive: Complete Learn to Play Manuals is a series designed to take the student from a beginner level through to an advanced standard of playing. All books are carefully graded and assume no prior knowledge on your behalf. Within the series many important aspects are covered, including learning to read notation and tablature, simple through to advanced technique, basic harmony, etc.

Progressive: Complete Learn to Play *Classical Guitar* Manual is to our knowledge the first comprehensive classical guitar method to incorporate **tablature** as an aid to **music notation** with the aim of learning the notes on the fingerboard as quickly and painlessly as possible. It has been my experience as a guitar teacher at all levels for many years, that the main contributing factor to the high rate of students discontinuing their studies is the frustration incurred due to the difficulty of learning to read traditional notation. For this reason I have included full tablature for a major portion of the method. This will help to overcome the reading difficulty and enable the student to play the music provided much quicker.

The student must, of course, be continually reading the notation in order to understand the timing required, and this subconsciously helps to collate the tab notes with the regular music notation. Eventually the tab should be phased out to leave the student with an ability to easily read notation, so important, as virtually all available classical guitar music is written only in notation. Obviously, **Progressive: Complete Teach Yourself *Classical Guitar*** can be used as a notation-only method by simply ignoring the tab.

As well as the thorough study of essential material pertaining to music theory, including a section on **harmony** and **basic technique**, the method also explores more advanced techniques such as **single, double and triple rest stroke thumb, rasgueado, silencing bass strings, tremolo, vibrato, harmonics** etc. in great detail. The learning of the fingerboard is explored via the study of **unison notes, movable Bar chords** etc., and the repertoire covers many periods featuring over 100 of the greatest studies and pieces written for the guitar. Importantly, **all** solo and duet pieces, as well as exercises, are recorded on the accompanying C.D.s.

ABOUT THE AUTHOR

Jason Waldron is one of Australia's most prominent classical guitarists. Studies in Australia were followed by master classes with Alirio Diaz, Oscar Caceres, Turibio Santos and John Williams. A recital in London's famed Wigmore Hall was followed by concerts and teaching in England and the U.S.A., including the American premiere of the Guillermo Flores Mendez Guitar Concerto with members of the Albuquerque Symphony Orchestra.

Jason's contribution to the development of the guitar in Australia has been considerable, particularly in the area of teaching and many of the countries leading guitarists have studied with him since the early 1970's. As one of the world's leading authors of guitar music, his involvement in publishing stretches from teaching material for L.T.P. Publishing to 3 volumes of guitar works by Agustin Barrios, several of which have been recorded by John Williams. For more information about Jason Waldron visit his website at:
www.jasonwaldron-guitarist.com.au

USING THE CDs *(Recorded by Cathy Waldron)*

It is recommended that you have a copy of the accompanying compact disc that includes all the examples in this book. The book shows you where to put your fingers and what technique to use and the recording lets you hear how each example should sound. Practice the examples slowly at first, gradually increasing tempo. Once you are confident you can play the example evenly without stopping the beat, try playing along with the recording. To play along with the CD your guitar must be in tune with it. If you have tuned using an electronic tuner (see below) your guitar will already be in tune with the CD. A small diagram of a compact disc with a number as shown below indicates a recorded example.

 **12.** ← CD Track Number

ELECTRONIC TUNER

The easiest and most accurate way to tune your guitar is by using an electronic tuner. An electronic tuner allows you to tune each string individually to the tuner, by indicating whether the notes are sharp (too high) or flat (too low). There are several types of electronic guitar tuners but most are relatively inexpensive and simple to operate. Tuning using other methods is difficult for beginner guitarists and it takes many months to master, so we

Electronic Tuner

recommend you purchase an electronic tuner, particularly if you do not have a guitar teacher or a friend who can tune it for you. Also if your guitar is way out of tune you can always take it to your local music store so they can tune it for you. Once a guitar has been tuned correctly it should only need minor adjustments before each practice session. **To learn to tune the guitar using other methods see Appendix One (page 202).**

TUNING YOUR GUITAR TO THE CD

Before you commence each lesson or practice session you will need to tune your guitar. If your guitar is out of tune everything you play will sound incorrect even though you are holding the correct notes. On the accompanying CD the **first six tracks** correspond to the **six strings of the guitar**. When playing along with duets, you will find that the first guitar part has been recorded on the left channel, while the second guitar part has been recorded on the right. This means you can use the stereo controls to hear either part separately or both parts together. A one bar click beat introduction is provided for each duet.

 6th String
E Note (Thickest string)

 5th String
A Note

 4th String
D Note

 3rd String
G Note

 2nd String
B Note

 1st String
E Note (Thinnest string)

THE CLASSICAL GUITAR

The classical guitar has nylon strings and a wider neck than the other types of guitar. It is most commonly used for playing Classical, Flamenco and Fingerstyles.

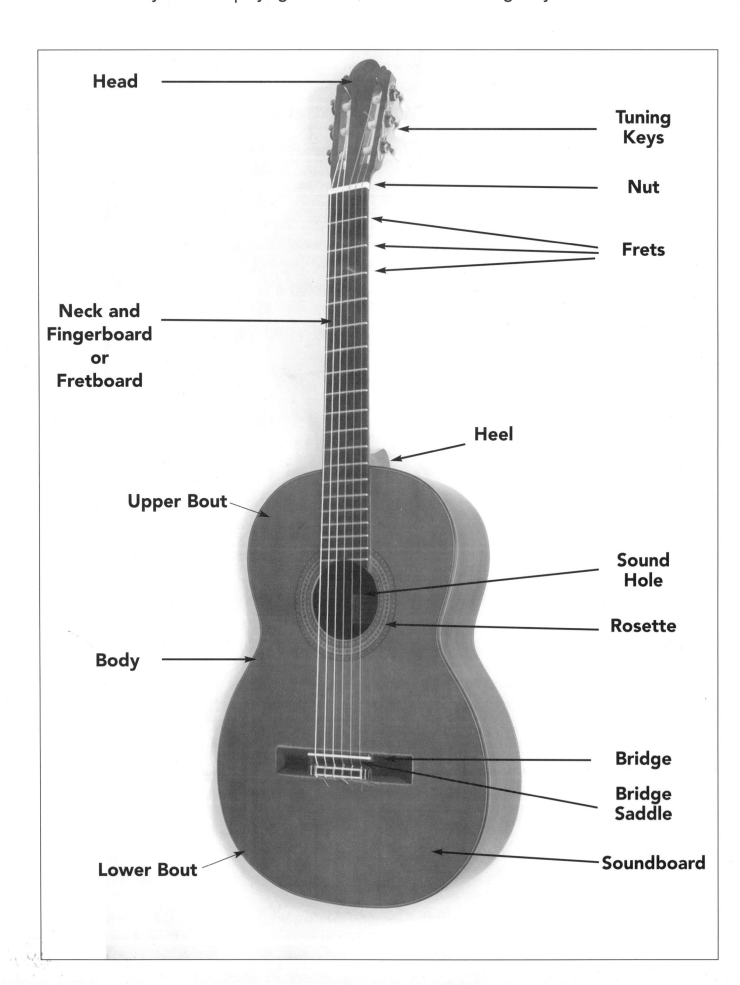

Head

Tuning Keys

Nut

Frets

Neck and Fingerboard or Fretboard

Heel

Upper Bout

Sound Hole

Rosette

Body

Bridge

Bridge Saddle

Lower Bout

Soundboard

HISTORY OF THE GUITAR

Although the guitar as we know it today is a relatively young instrument, the history of its predecessors stretches back several thousand years.

The Assyrians, Persians, Chaldeans and Hebrews all had versions of plucked stringed instruments and an instrument called the rebec was brought to Spain with the Moorish invasion in 711.

Many changes took place over the years but by the late 18th century the guitar shape had developed into the 6 stringed instrument we know today, as opposed to the smaller 4 and 5 string versions popular during the 17th century.

It was early in the 19th century that several great figures appeared in Spain and Italy who were to establish the guitar as a respected concert instrument.
The greatest of these was Fernando Sor who was born in Barcelona, Spain in 1778. Throughout his lifetime (he died in 1839) Sor played concerts, taught and composed hundreds of works for guitar including studies for beginners through to virtuoso pieces played by most concert guitarists today. Such was his talent and high standing in the musical world that the French music critic Fetis called him the 'Beethoven of the guitar'.

Notable contemporaries of Sor included his friend and duet partner Dionisio Aguado (born Madrid 1784, died 1849) who wrote many short attractive pieces and studies, and the Italians Ferdinand Carulli (1792-1853) Matteo Carcassi (1770-1828) and Mauro Giuliani (1781-1829).
All were great virtuosi who enriched the guitar's repertoire and, most importantly, wrote methods to further its development.

Unfortunately the guitar lost popularity after this period and it wasn't revived until the late 19th century through the efforts of Francisco Tarrega in Spain and Agustin Barrios in South America.
Tarrega (1854-1909), although born into a poor family, overcame great hardship to become a virtuoso player and composer for his beloved instrument, developing along the way the basis of the modern technique which is used by today's guitarists.
Barrios (born in Paraguay 1885, died El Salvador 1944) was a supreme virtuoso who expanded upon the work of Tarrega in both a technical and compositional sense and became known as the 'Paganini of the guitar' because of his astounding playing ability. Interestingly, Barrios was the first guitarist to make gramophone recordings.
One of Tarrega's students, Miguel Llobet, carried on the work of his master in the first half of this century and he in turn was a big influence, through inspiration, on the illustrious career of Andres Segovia.

Through his untiring work over more than 70 years, Segovia (1894-1987) has acquired a respectability for the guitar which has assured its place as a serious classical instrument.

The great concert guitarists of today, including Alirio Diaz, John Williams and Julian Bream carry on the tradition of the earlier masters and through their concerts, recordings and teaching, assure a healthy future for the classical guitar.

HOW TO READ MUSIC

There are two methods used to write guitar music. First is the **traditional music notation** method (using music notes, ♩) and second is **tablature.** Both are used in this book. Whilst most guitarists find tablature easier to read, it is imperative to learn to read traditional music notation as has been explained in the introduction.

TABLATURE

Tablature is a method of indicating the position of notes on the fretboard. There are six "tab" lines each representing one of the six strings of the guitar. Study the following diagram.

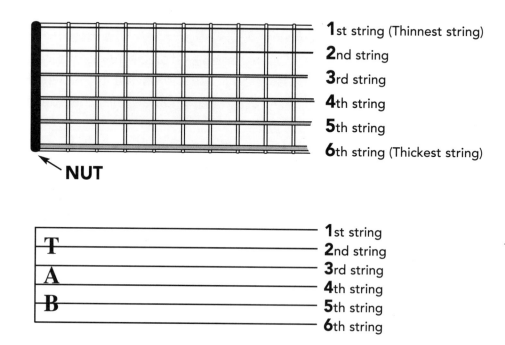

1st string (Thinnest string)
2nd string
3rd string
4th string
5th string
6th string (Thickest string)

NUT

1st string
2nd string
3rd string
4th string
5th string
6th string

When a number is placed on one of the lines, it indicates the fret location of a note e.g.

This indicates the open 3rd string (a G note).

This indicates the 3rd fret of the 5th string (a C note).

This indicates the 1st fret of the 1st string (an F note).

MUSIC NOTATION

The musical alphabet consists of 7 letters:

A B C D E F G

Music is written on a **staff**, which consists of 5 parallel lines between which there are 4 spaces.

MUSIC STAFF

TREBLE CLEF

The treble or 'G' clef is placed at the beginning of each staff line. This clef indicates the position of the note G. (It is an old fashioned method of writing the letter G, with the centre of the clef being written on the second staff line.)

Treble or 'G' Clef →

G note

The other lines and spaces on the staff are named as such:

Extra notes can be added by the use of short lines, called **leger lines**.

When a note is placed on the staff its **head** indicates its position, e.g.:

head   stem

This is a G note

This is a C note

When the note head is below the middle staff line the stem points upward (to the right) and when the head is above the middle line the stem points downward (to the left). A note placed on the middle line (**B**) can have its stem pointing either up or down.

BAR LINES

Bar lines are drawn across the staff, which divides the music into sections called **bars** or **measures**. A **double bar line** (thick and thin line) signifies either the end of the music, or the end of an important section of it.

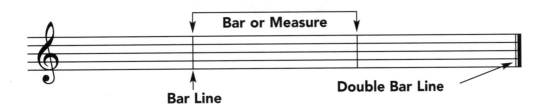

Bar or Measure

Bar Line

Double Bar Line

NOTE VALUES

The table below sets out the most common notes used in music and their respective time values (i.e. length of time held). For each note value there is an equivalent rest, which indicates a period of silence.

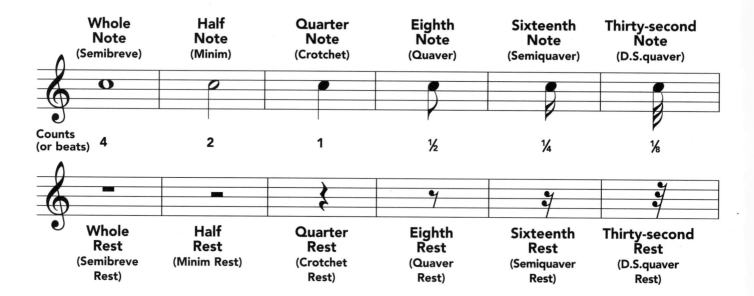

	Whole Note (Semibreve)	Half Note (Minim)	Quarter Note (Crotchet)	Eighth Note (Quaver)	Sixteenth Note (Semiquaver)	Thirty-second Note (D.S.quaver)
Counts (or beats)	4	2	1	½	¼	⅛
	Whole Rest (Semibreve Rest)	Half Rest (Minim Rest)	Quarter Rest (Crotchet Rest)	Eighth Rest (Quaver Rest)	Sixteenth Rest (Semiquaver Rest)	Thirty-second Rest (D.S.quaver Rest)

DOTTED NOTES

If a **dot** is placed after a note it increases the value of that note by half. e.g.

Dotted Half Note   𝅗𝅥•   **(2 + 1) = 3 counts**

Dotted Quarter Note   ♩•   **(1 + ½) = 1½ counts**

Dotted Whole Note   𝅝•   **(4 + 2) = 6 counts**

TIED NOTES

A **tie** is a curved line joining two or more notes of the same pitch, where the second note(s) **is not played** but its time value is added to that of the first note. Here are two examples:

2   +   1 = 3 counts   **4   +   2 + 1 = 7 counts**

In both of these examples only the first note is played.

TIME SIGNATURES

At the beginning of each piece of music, after the treble clef, is the **time signature**.

Time Signature
(pronounced Four Four time)

4 – this indicates 4 beats per bar.

4 – this indicates that each beat is worth a quarter note (crotchet).

The time signature indicates the number of beats per bar (the top number) and the type of note receiving one beat (the bottom number). For example:

In $\frac{4}{4}$ time there must be the equivalent of 4 quarter note beats per bar, e.g.

COMMON TIME (𝄴)

$\frac{4}{4}$ is the most common time signature and is sometimes represented by this symbol called **common time**.

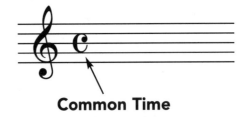

Common Time

THREE FOUR TIME ($\frac{3}{4}$)

Another time signature often used is **three four time** (written $\frac{3}{4}$).

$\frac{3}{4}$ indicates 3 quarter note beats per bar, e.g.

SITTING POSITION
IMPORTANT RULES

It is most important for you to always practice with the same chair and footstool height and to place the footstool approx. 6" (15cm) away from the left leg of the chair. Always sit on the front edge to avoid knocking the lower bout of the guitar against the chair (see **photo A**). The chair and footstool height should enable your left thigh to slope down at a slight angle towards the body (see **photo A**). The left leg should be at right angles to the floor (see **photo B**) and should not be allowed to be pushed away by the guitar.

Viewed from the side (see **photo A**) the back should be straight, head relaxed and not leaning forward over the guitar. Viewed from the front (see **photo B**), the body should be straight and upright, the guitar resting at approx. 40 degree to the floor so that the head of the guitar is just below eye level but not too horizontal.

SITTING POSITION

photo A: left leg has slight downward slope (as indicated by dotted line).

photo B: points of contact
Note: adjustable footstool commercially available.

If you follow the rules outlined above, the guitar will be supported in four positions:

1. the left leg (raised)
2. the right leg
3. the right arm (on the lower bout)
4. the right side of the chest

The correct sitting position will provide a fixed position for the guitar and allow complete freedom of movement for the left arm.

Viewed from above (see **diag.**) the guitar must be placed at a right angle to the left leg. Your upper body should be turned slightly to the left from the waist, to enable the upper bout of the guitar to rest against the right side only of your chest, and not flat against it.

This is vitally important as only this position will allow total freedom of movement for the left arm and hand.

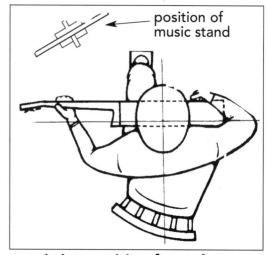

sitting position from above

RIGHT HAND NOTATION

The right hand fingers are named such:

p (pulgar) - **thumb**
i (indicio) - **index finger**
m (medio) - **middle finger**
a (annular) - **ring finger**

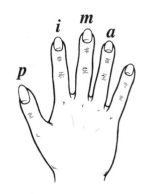

The little finger is not used in classical guitar playing.

right hand notation

RIGHT HAND FINGERNAILS

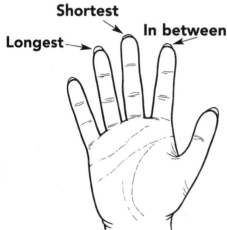

It is widely accepted that the right hand fingernails be used to pluck the strings as this will give a greater control over the volume and tone of the notes you play. It is therefore assumed that you use nails for the duration of this method. If, however, for one reason or another nails cannot be grown or kept, you will have to focus attention on the fingertips in place of the nails. Nail length and shape is mainly dependant on personal preference but the most common shape is that which follows the curve of the finger-tip. Experimentation and listening for the best tone over a long period is advised.

Remember, the nails are to the guitarist what the stylus is to a record player and must be looked after accordingly. They should be filed and shaped regularly, working from the underside of the nail (Use very fine 'wet or dry' sandpaper).

RIGHT ARM PLACEMENT

In dealing with correct right hand position, you must first consider the right arm and its relaxation and resting place on the guitar's body.

The right arm must be considered a dead weight, i.e., shoulder relaxed with the arm resting on the front edge of the guitar just forward of the elbow joint. Allowing for slight differences in arm length, the forearm rests on a point just backward of an imaginary line drawn from the bridge as seen in the photo. With the arm in this position, the right hand is now ready to be placed in its playing position.

forearm resting point

right arm placement

RIGHT HAND POSITION

Having established a comfortable sitting position and arm placement, you should proceed as follows. Allow the right hand to relax at the wrist as a dead weight. The most natural and common position for the knuckles is to follow a line almost parallel to, and directly over, the bass strings (see **photo A**).

The top of the wrist should be slightly arched to follow a parallel plain with the soundboard (see **photo B**).

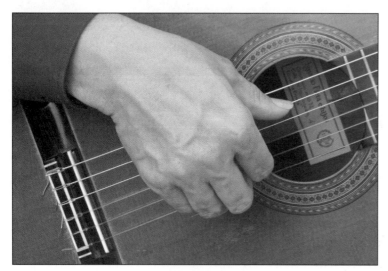

photo A

photo B

METHOD OF PLACEMENT

Place *a* on the 1st string so that it is perpendicular to the string (see **photo C**).

Place *p* on the 6th string at an angle of 45° to the string, thus forming a right angle triangle (see **photo D**).

Finally, place *i* and *m* on the 3rd and 2nd strings respectively, allowing them to slope into-wards *a* (see **photo E**).

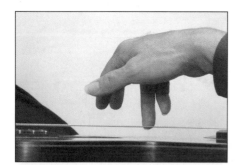

photo C: *a* finger placement

photo D: *p* placement

photo E: *i* and *m* placement

Note that the fingers are **not straight** but are **gently curved** (see **photo B**) and that the thumb is **straight** and extended away from the fingers (see **photo A**).

Assuming that the fingernails are filed and ready for use as described earlier, you should make sure that each finger **grips** its string firmly between the flesh and nail. This 'gripping' is vitally important and you should regard it, together with the above hand position, as a starting point for all right hand technique.

FINGER PLUCKING ACTION

1. REST STROKE (*i, m, a*)
(used mainly for single line and melody playing)

photo A: rest stroke preparation

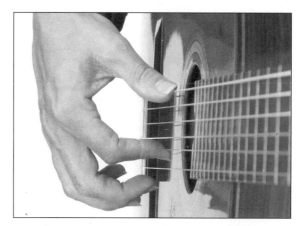

photo B: rest stroke completion

THE REST STROKE

The **rest stroke** (indicated by ▽), is so named because the finger, having plucked the gripped string, comes to rest temporarily against the adjacent string.

Grip *i* on the first string, making sure the right hand is correctly positioned (see **photo A**).

Pluck the first string by allowing the tip joint to collapse and come to rest on the second string on the flesh approx. ¼" (6mm) from the fingertip (see **photo B**).

Relax the tip and allow *i* to return to a position close to (but not touching) the first string, ready to strike again. Repeat this exercise with *m* and *a*, remembering to keep the right hand as still as possible.

Note: More detailed rest stroke information appears later in the method.

ALTERNATION

In order to achieve speed and evenness, both vital for later development, you must practice alternating right hand finger combinations in scale and single line melodies. Each of the exercises to follow should be played first with *im*, then *ma*, then *ia*.

A very important aspect pf right hand finger action during rest stroke passages is for the fingers to perform a walking motion. As *i* plucks, *m* is close to the string and ready to strike. As *i* springs away after resting on the adjacent string (previously explained) *m* proceeds to strike while *i* waits to start over again. Used continuously this sets up the 'walking' action known as **alternation**.

LEFT HAND NOTATION

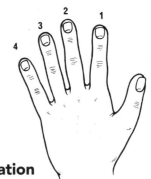

1. First finger (index)
2. Second finger (middle)
3. Third finger (ring)
4. Fourth finger (little)

left hand notation

LEFT HAND POSITION AND FINGER PLACEMENT

Bring the left hand to the fingerboard and place the fingers on the first string as shown in **photos A** and **B**. Your fingers should be **on their tips** and placed directly **behind** the frets (not on top of them).

photo A

photo B

Notice how the fingers are separated to allow access to the first four frets. Also in **photo A**, how the wrist is quite flat and the left hand is angled away from the fretboard for the fourth finger (dotted indication). Notice also how the fingers assume an almost square shape for maximum strength and to allow each finger to bridge over adjacent strings without touching them.

LEFT HAND THUMB

The left hand thumb should remain under the first finger, pressing on its ball in the middle of the neck, as shown in **photo C**. This makes finger stretches easier and more comfortable. Even if the first finger is not being used, this 'relative' position should be maintained (see **photo D**). Later on as the hand moves up the fretboard, it is necessary to maintain the thumb under the first finger at all times.

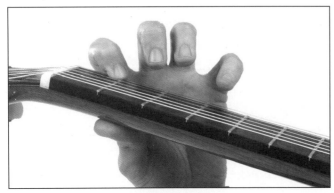

photo C

photo D

SECTION 1

LESSON ONE

FIRST STRING NOTES (OR NOTES ON ①) *

Note: An **open string** meaning a string not depressed by a left hand finger when played is indicated as **0**.

*Note: a number in a circle indicates the string.

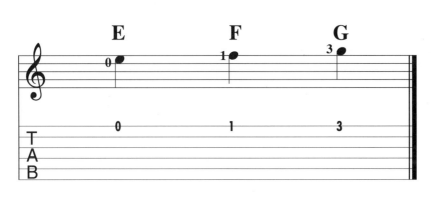

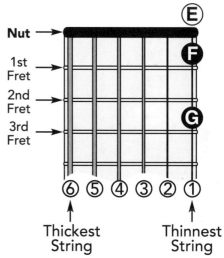

THE FIRST POSITION

As can be seen above, the first finger (1) is used to play the F note on the first fret, first string (①), and this constitutes the **first position** which applies whenever 1 is used on the first fret of any string.

As described on page 18, place your fingers **on their tips**, immediately **behind** the frets and **press hard** to avoid buzzing or deadened notes. Notice how the tip segments stand almost perpendicular to the string for strength and to avoid touching adjacent strings. Make sure to **alternate**, first using *im*, then *ma*, then *ia*, remembering to flex tip joints. Rest the thumb (*p*) on a lower bass string (i.e. ⑥) to keep the right hand steady.

The above and following examples use **quarter notes** (or **crotchets**) ♩, worth **one count each** and introduce ¼ time, where there are **four quarter note beats per bar**.

Note: Exercises, studies and pieces to follow in the method have been recorded in an "academic" rather than a freer musical style for purposes of demonstration.
Note: Exercises, studies and pieces to follow do not indicate **tempo** (speed) until page 105, and should be practiced at a comfortable tempo by each individual student.

7.

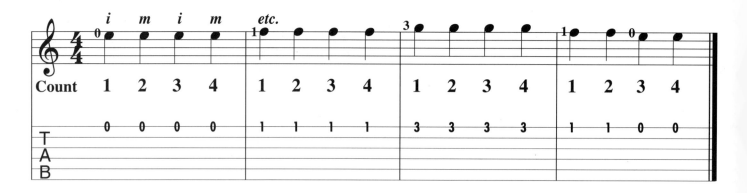

8.

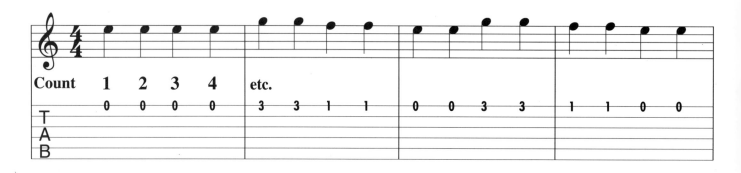

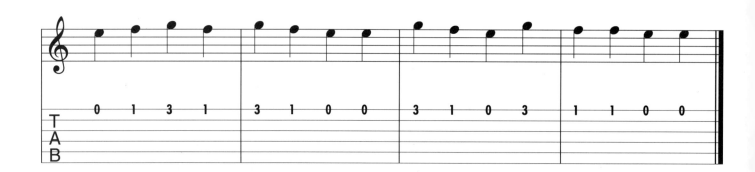

SAYING THE NAMES OF THE NOTES AND COUNTING

It is extremely important for the student to read through, saying the names of the notes of each new study or piece, before attempting to play. Similarly, as each piece is played, the student should either say the names of the notes or count the notes in each bar, as shown above. It is also invaluable to write out (on music manuscript paper) each piece as it is studied throughout the method, as this greatly helps to reinforce the learning process.

SECOND STRING NOTES (OR NOTES ON ②)

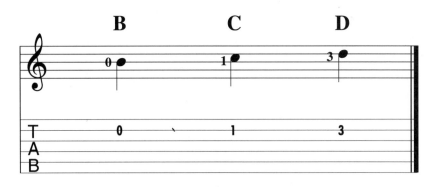 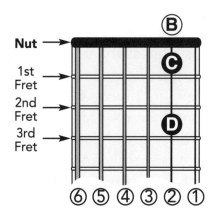

 **9.**

Ex. 9 introduces the **half-note** (or **minim**) ♩, which is worth **two counts**.

Two quarter notes equal one half note i.e. ♩ + ♩ = ♩

In bar 8 the half notes are played on the first and third beats, as indicated by the count.

This example is 8 bars long. Bar numbers are the small numbers written below the staff.

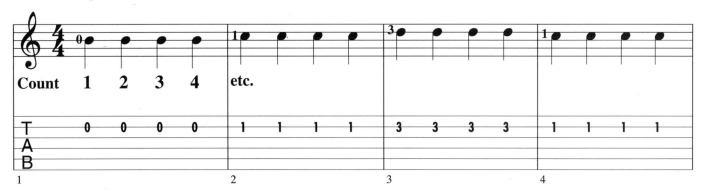

CHECKLIST

- Make sure your guitar is in tune (page 7).
- **Watch the music**, not your fingers.
- Concentrate on learning the notes, rather than memorising the piece. To do this, you should play very slowly, naming each note as you play it.
- Remember to use the correct fingering: **first** finger for **first** fret notes, and **third** finger for **third** fret notes.
- Alternate right hand fingers.

CROSSING STRINGS

When moving between two or more strings, i.e. ① - ② - ① etc., it is necessary to make a slight arm adjustment using the right elbow as a pivot point (see dotted indication). This adjustment allows the right hand fingers to pluck consistently on each string without changing hand position and finger action.

This movement equals the width between 2 strings.

DUETS

It is important for you to be able to play with other musicians and the best practice for this is the study of **duets** (See page 7 to play along with CD).

Playing duets will present specific problems. Be careful of the following:
- Make sure to stay on your correct part (e.g. the top or bottom line).
- Pay particular attention to your timing and try not to stop if the other guitarist makes a mistake.
- Do not be distracted by the other guitarist's part.

The following duets make use of the six notes which you have so far studied.

Duet part notated as T (Teacher). Remember to alternate.

Note: A one bar click track introduction is provided for each duet.

CD 1 — 10. Ode to Joy (Duet)

Beethoven

11. Skip To My Lou (Duet)

Try playing the following familiar tune using previous fingerings without the aid of TAB.

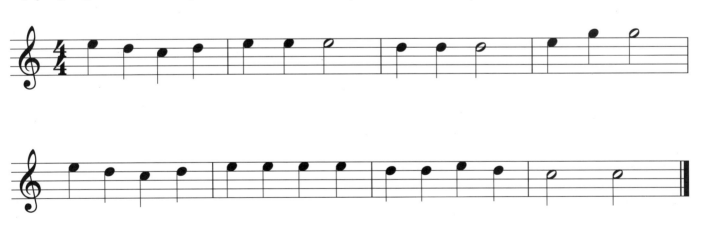

Note: The student can now begin to use **Repertoire Book 1**, Part 1.

24

Jingle Bells introduces the **whole note** (or **semibreve**) **o** in bars 4,12 and 16 which is worth **four counts**. Four quarter notes or two half notes equal one whole note.

i.e. ♩ + ♩ + ♩ + ♩ = **o** , ♩ + ♩ = **o**

It is played on the first beat and held for the remaining three as indicated by the count.

12. Jingle Bells (Duet)

LESSON TWO

THIRD STRING NOTES (OR NOTES ON ③)

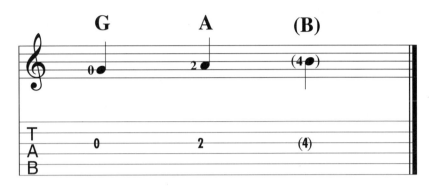

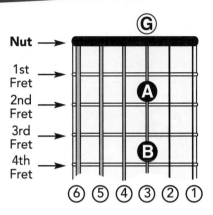

Note: Use of 4th finger on B (③) which is the same note as B (②) open and can be substituted at any time.

You now have two **G** notes; the one above and the one at the third fret on the first string. This type of repetition occurs with all notes, since the musical alphabet goes from **A** to **G**, and then back to **A** again. The distance between the two **G** notes is called an **octave** (see **Note Summary** below).

The following exercise is in $\frac{2}{4}$ time. $\frac{2}{4}$ **time** indicates **two quarter note beats per bar** (it is rhythmically similar to $\frac{4}{4}$ time).

It also introduces the tie, which is not played, but its time value is added to that of the note before it. The tie is indicated as ⌣ or ⌢ (see page 12).

13.

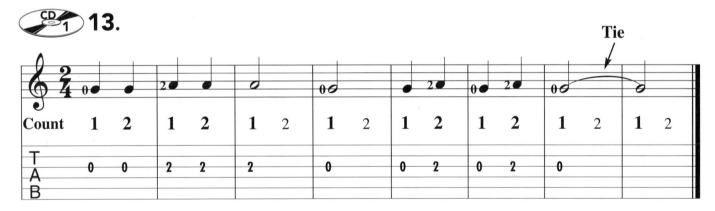

NOTE SUMMARY (one octave G-G)

3RD STRING NOTES		2ND STRING NOTES			1ST STRING NOTES		
G	A	B	C	D	E	F	G
Fret 0	2	0	1	3	0	1	3
Fingering 0	2	0	1	3	0	1	3

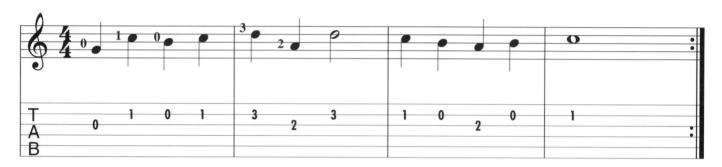

14. Aura Lee

Aura Lee introduces the **music repeat sign** (**Bar 4**), which consists of a **double bar line, with two dots placed before them**. It indicates a repeat of the section of music which has just been played. The repeat sign in the final bar of line one indicates that the piece must then be repeated from the beginning through to the end of line three.
Remember to adjust the right arm (page 22) to accommodate ① , ② and ③.

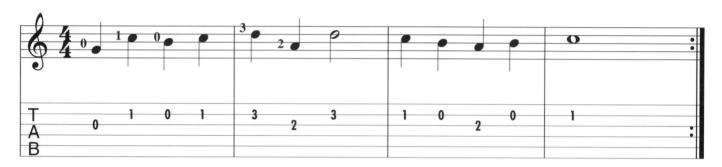

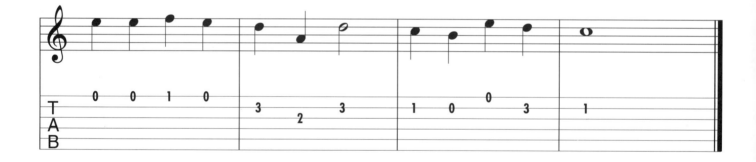

15. Avignon (Duet)

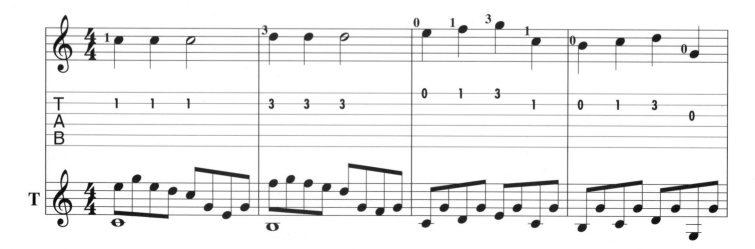

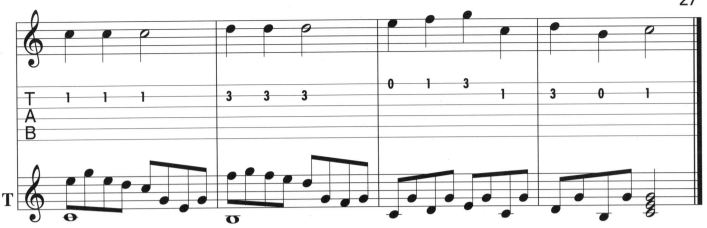

 16. **Michael Row the Boat Ashore** (Duet)

This piece introduces **lead-in notes** (also called **anacrusis**), which are notes occurring before the first complete bar of music. In this case, 2 quarter notes should be played on counts three and four of the count-in (as indicated). You will notice that the final bar of the piece contains only one half note (two counts), which acts as a 'balance' to the lead-in notes. This is quite common, but does not always occur.

The following pieces introduce the **eighth note** (or **quaver**) ♪, which is worth **half a beat**. Two eighth notes equal one quarter note i.e. ♪ ♪ = ♩ or, more commonly written as ♫ = ♩ . The line joining the two eighth notes is called a **ligature**.

The plus sign (+) is used to count groups of eighth notes, as indicated in bars 5 and 6. In pronunciation say 'and' e.g.

```
        1   +   2   +
Say:   one and two and
```

17. Frere Jacques (Duet)

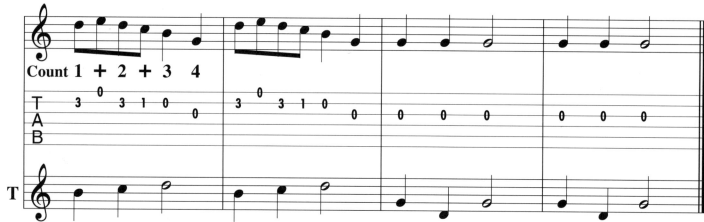

* Note: Try substituting 4th finger on B③ (see page 25).

18. Study (Duet)

Giuliani

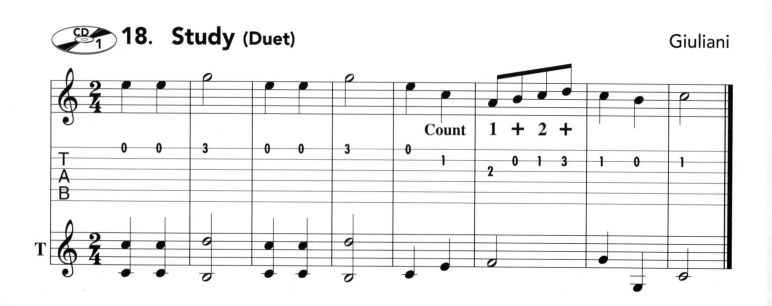

The following pieces introduce $\frac{3}{4}$ **time**, where there are **three quarter note beats per bar** (see page 13).

Note: Anacrusis, in this case 1 quarter note.

Note: Use of 4 as substitute for 3 on G① and D② .

 19. Ash Grove

 20. Away in a Manger

The following piece introduces the **dotted quarter note** ♩. which is **worth 1 1/2 counts**. When a dot is placed after a note it **increases the value of that note by half** (see page 12). When a dotted note is followed by an eighth note the count is as follows:

Count: 1 2 + 3

Note that a **dot** can be used in a similar way as the **tie**. i.e.

Dotted Rhythm   **Tied Rhythm**

Count: 1 2 + 3 4   Count: 1   2 + 3   4

Mary had a Little Lamb ————— Dotted Quarter Note

Tie

Note: Several examples of familiar dotted quarter note melodies are available in **Complete Learn to Play Classical Guitar Repertoire Book 1** and recorded on the accompanying CD.

LESSON THREE

THUMB PLUCKING ACTION

1. FREE STROKE (*p*)

In the following exercises the thumb (*p*) will be playing the open bass notes written below.

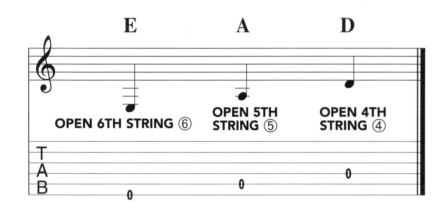

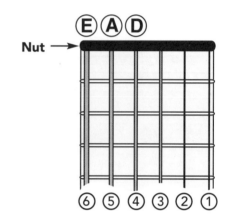

Just as *p* rested on the 6th string (⑥) for support during exercises on ①, ② and ③, so should *i*, *m* and *a* grip the third, second and first strings respectively during the following examples. Use a **circular motion** as illustrated in **photo A** and be sure to exercise the entire length of the thumb from its base (see **photo B**). The thumb must not bend when making its stroke, and should pick with a downward motion, striking the string before passing freely over the adjacent string (hence the term **free stroke**) and returning to its starting position.

photo A

photo B

 21.   Use *p* throughout.

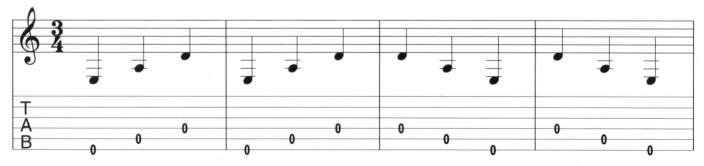

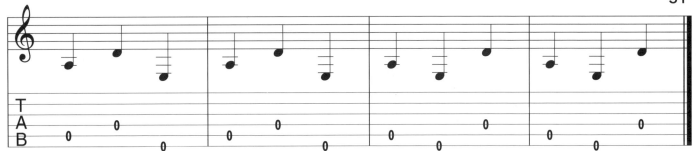

FOURTH STRING NOTES *(OR NOTES ON ④)*

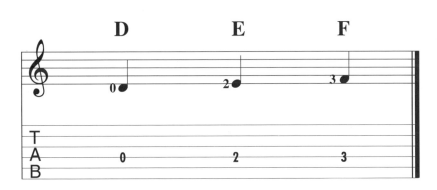

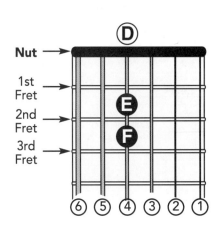

RE-EXAMINING LEFT HAND POSITION

Notice **how the first finger rests against the fingerboard** in the following photos (B and D). This is standard procedure when playing on ④, ⑤, and ⑥ as it allows the left hand to remain close to the fingerboard and the fingers to play with a similar action to that on ①, ② and ③. The first finger (and the whole left hand), should move progressively closer to the fingerboard from ① to ② to ③, until it rests against it when playing on ④ (see **photos**). Note how the hand angles away for the fourth finger as explained on pg. 18.

photo A: first finger on ①

photo B: first finger on ④

photo C: first finger on ①

photo D: first finger on ④

THE RESTS

The following example (Ex. 22) introduces the **quarter note rest** ‿ (bar 4) which is used to indicate a period of silence. For each note value there is a corresponding rest, as outlined in the following table.

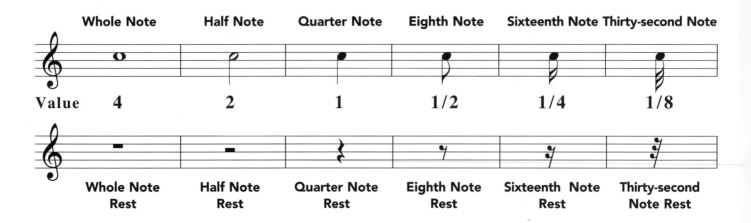

Whole Note	Half Note	Quarter Note	Eighth Note	Sixteenth Note	Thirty-second Note
4	2	1	1/2	1/4	1/8
Whole Note Rest	Half Note Rest	Quarter Note Rest	Eighth Note Rest	Sixteenth Note Rest	Thirty-second Note Rest

It also introduces the **dotted half note** ⌐. (bar 8) which is **worth three counts**. When a dot is placed after a note it **increases the value of that note by a half** (see page 12).

CD 1   22.   Use *p* throughout.

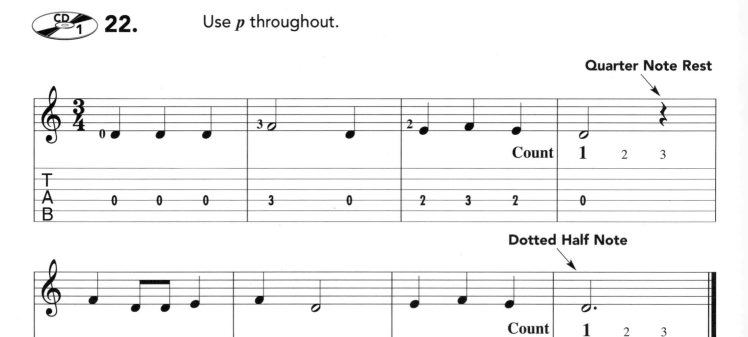

LESSON FOUR

FINGER PLUCKING ACTION

2. FREE STROKE (*i, m, a*)
(used primarily for chords and arpeggios)

The **free stroke** is so named because the finger, having plucked one string, passes freely over the neighbouring string. The sound is produced by the nail only. The finger should move across the string, rather than pull out from it. This movement will enable the hand to remain steady (i.e. only the fingers move).

With the right hand in correct position and **fingers gripping the strings** as described on page 16, pluck the 3rd string with *i* (see **photos A** and **B**). Leave *p, m* and *a* gripping the 6th, 2nd and 1st strings for support and steadiness.

Note: Free stroke will be studied in more detail later in the method.

photo A: free stroke preparation *i*

photo B: free stroke completion *i*

Repeat this procedure for *m* and *a*.

Make sure to retain correct hand position by checking **photos A** and **B** on page 16. The notes you have just played are written below.

Remember that a **number in a circle** i.e. ③ indicates the **third string**.

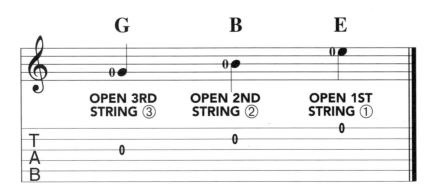

OPEN STRING FREE STROKE EXERCISES

In the following examples rest *p* on the 6th string for support.
Practice **strongly**, only use small finger movements i.e. at no time should the fingers be more than 1/2" (13mm) from their respective strings.

 **23.**

TWO AND MORE NOTES PLAYED TOGETHER

The following example in $\frac{4}{4}$ time, involves two and three open string notes played together. Use the same procedure as previously outlined on page 33. Be sure to keep both (or all) fingers together at the tips and make the notes sound as one.

Two or more notes played together are generally called **chords**. The subject of chords will be dealt with in more detail later in the method.

 **24.0**

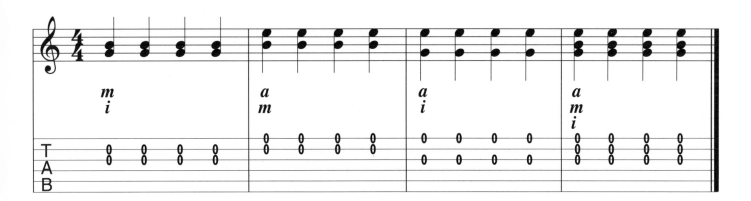

 **24.1 Waltz**

The following **Waltz** (a dance in $\frac{3}{4}$ timing) uses open strings in all but bars 2 and 6 where it is necessary to place 1 and 2 together on the notes C ② and A ③.

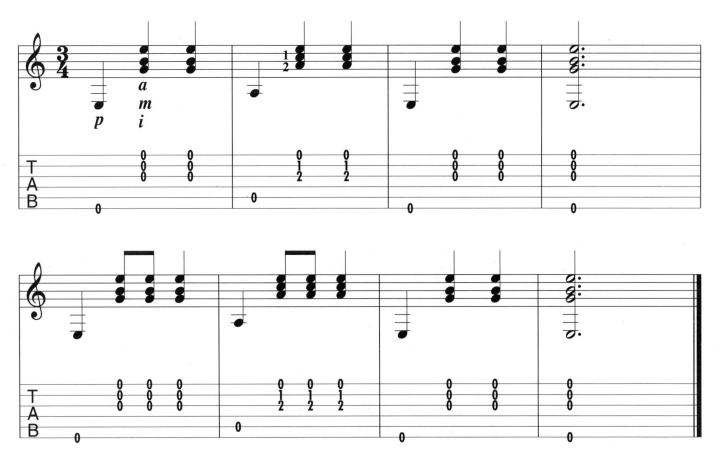

RIGHT HAND INDEPENDENCE EXERCISES

The following examples are invaluable in establishing an independence between the thumb and fingers of the right hand.

Grip *i*, *m* and *a* on the third, second and first strings respectively, making sure the right hand is correctly positioned and relaxed.

 **25.**

1. Pluck the sixth, fifth and fourth string with *p* (free stroke) as notated, using the plucking action as described on page 30.

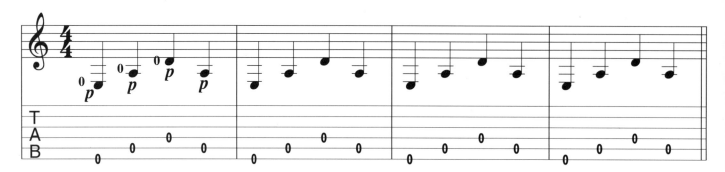

2. Without stopping, add *i*, *m* and *a* free stroke. The action of the thumb must not change.

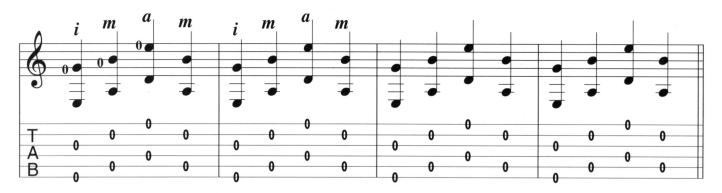

3. Again, without stopping *p*, add the chords below.

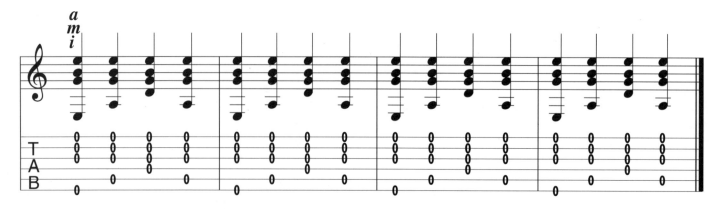

Practice slowly and strongly. At this stage it would be beneficial to return to **lesson one** and re-do all examples and studies to this point using **free stroke fingers**.

LESSON FIVE

COMBINING FINGERS AND THUMB

Having learned the notes on ① ② ③ and ④, it is now possible to combine **free stroke fingers** with **free stroke thumb** in the following pieces.

They are essentially single line pieces, but the use of free stroke and the open ④ provide a full harmonic sound.

 26. Bells of Big Ben

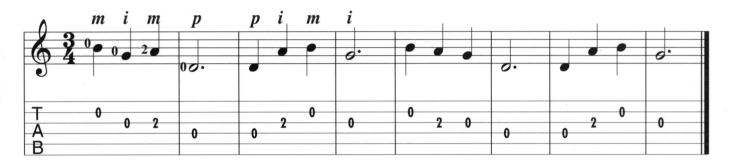

The next pieces introduce the idea of **voices** or **parts**. The **upper voice** note stems point **upwards** and the **lower voice** note stems point **downwards**. This is standard practice in order to differentiate between more than one part and create the sound called **polyphony** or **many voices** - in these examples, two voices.

Note that the tie gives a truer indication of time value than the above example, however both types of writing are common in guitar music. The quarter note rest (𝄽), bar 1, only applies to the lower voice.

 27. Go Tell Aunt Rhody

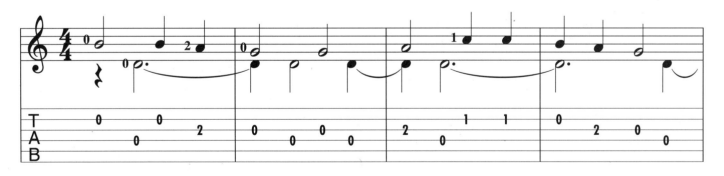

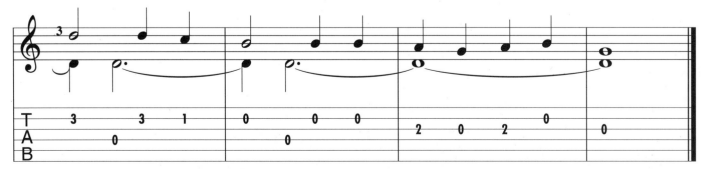

Note: The student can now begin to use *Repertoire Book 1*, Part 2.

28. Old Kentucky Home Foster

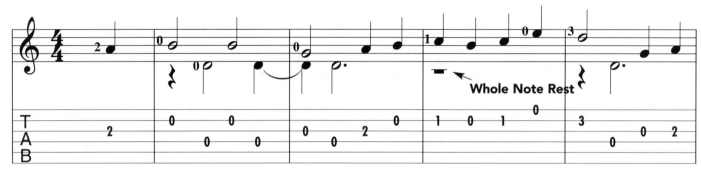

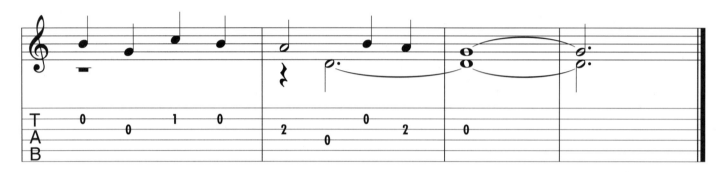

Try playing the following familiar melody using fingering as in the previous three pieces without TAB.

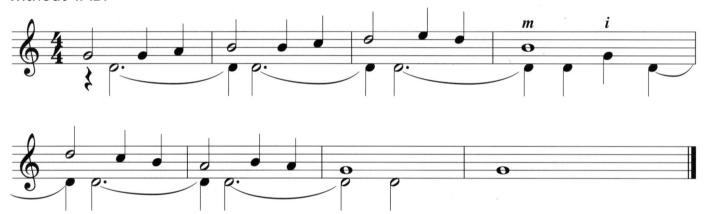

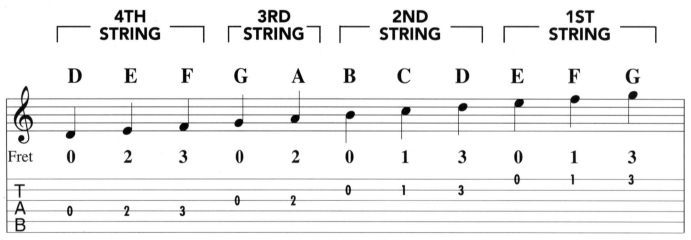

NOTE SUMMARY

	4TH STRING			3RD STRING		2ND STRING			1ST STRING		
	D	E	F	G	A	B	C	D	E	F	G
Fret	0	2	3	0	2	0	1	3	0	1	3

CHECKLIST

- Remember to maintain correct left and right hand playing positions (see photos on page 16 and 18) and sit in front of a mirror to study from other angles.
- **Count** as you play, and be particularly careful of dotted notes and ties. You may also find it advantageous to tap your foot with the beat.

LESSON SIX

FIFTH STRING NOTES (OR NOTES ON ⑤)

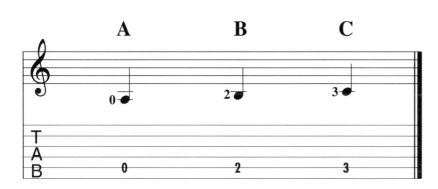

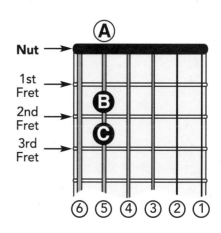

CD 1 **29.**

The **C** at the beginning of this exercise stands for **common time**, which is another name for **4/4** time.

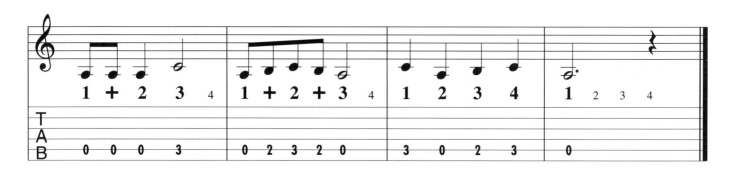

Note: The student can now begin to use **Repertoire Book 1**, Part 3.

30. **Volga Boatman** This piece combines notes on ④ and ⑤.

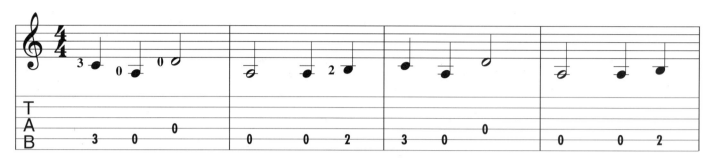

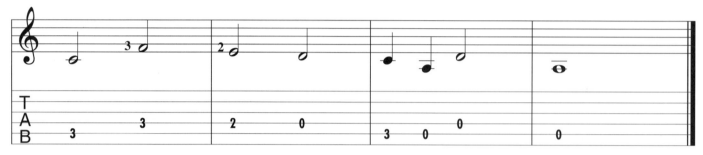

31. **Harem Dance**

This piece combines *p* free stroke with *i m* free stroke. It also introduces the whole and half note rests (see page 32).

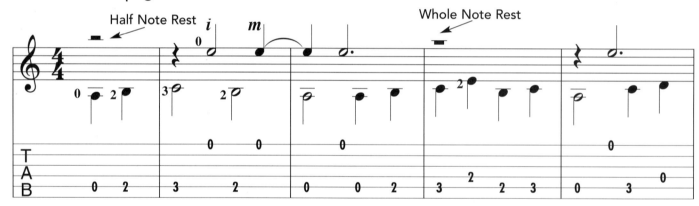

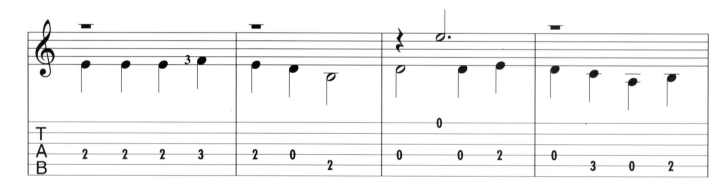

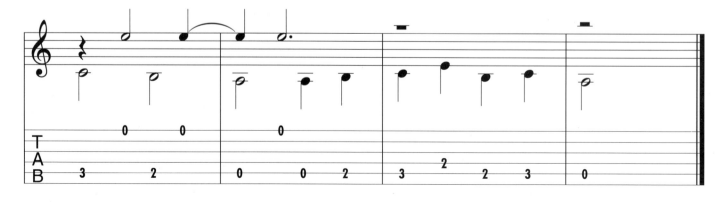

TWO NOTES PLAYED TOGETHER
THUMB (*p*) AND INDEX FINGER (*i*) RELATIONSHIP

photo A
Prior to plucking ④ (*p*)
and ③ (*i*).

photo B
After plucking ④ (*p*) and ③ (*i*).

photo C
After plucking ④ (*p*) and ③ (*i*).

Be sure to observe correct right hand position and allow *p* to come together lightly with *i* (**photo B**) on adjacent strings to form a "cross" (**photo C**).

The following piece introduces **first** and **second endings**. On the first time through, ending one is played as indicated by the bracket; (⌐1⌐).
The piece is then repeated from the beginning (as indicated by the repeat sign), but is replaced by ending two, as indicated by the bracket; (⌐2⌐). Be sure not to play both endings together.

32. Chopsticks

Lulli

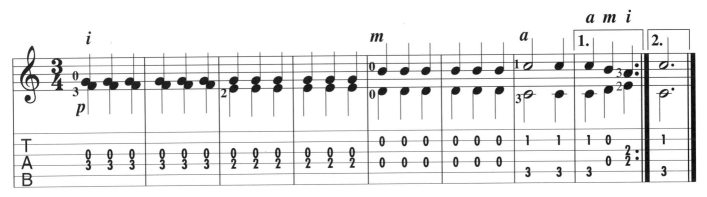

NOTE SUMMARY

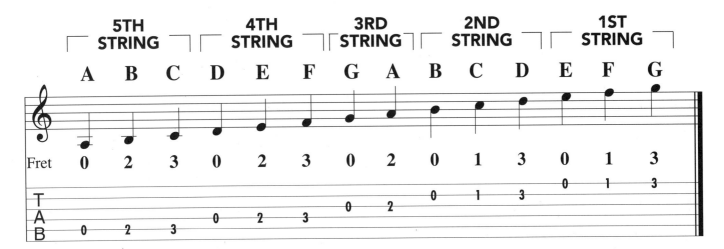

SIXTH STRING NOTES (OR NOTES ON ⑥)

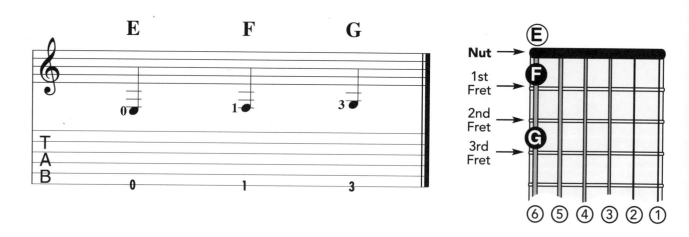

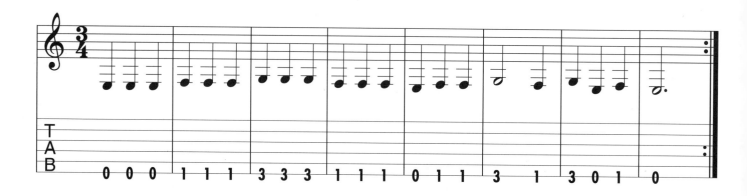

33.

34. Volga Boatman

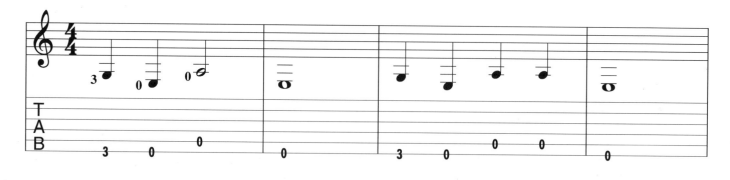

35. Slavonic Dance (Duet)

Dvorak

A full arrangement of the **Slavonic Dance** is available in *Popular Classics of the Great Composers Vol.4* by Jason Waldron (LTP Publishing - visit **www.learntoplaymusic.com**).

NOTE SUMMARY

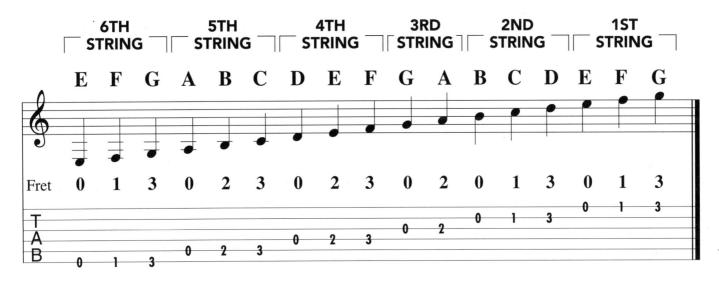

 **36. Asturias**

Albeniz

This piece combines notes on ④ ⑤ and ⑥. Use left hand fingerings as practiced previously. Alternate *pipm* etc. It also introduces the **Eighth Note Rest**. Concentrate on reading the **notation**.

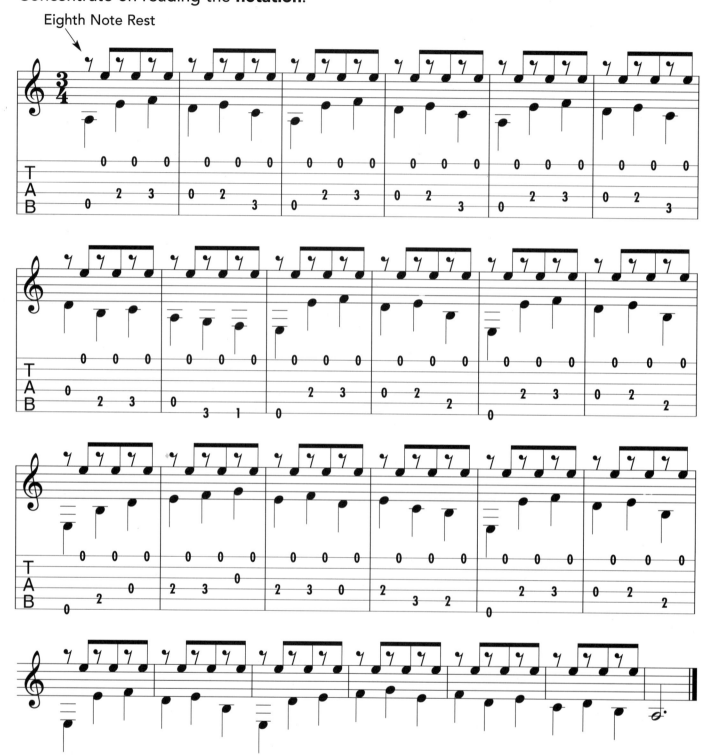

IMPORTANT NOTE

It will be observed that for the duration of the method, TAB will sometimes be omitted when it is felt that sufficient collation has been provided between notation and TAB to allow the student to read the notation only.

Occasionally, the TAB lines are left blank to be completed by the student.

Eventually, all TAB will be phased out.

Note: The student can now begin to use **Repertoire Book 1**, Part 4.

OPEN POSITION NOTES

Also incorporating the **first position**, see page 19.

All of the notes you have studied, as summarised below, are in the **open position**. The **open position** consists of the **open string notes** and the notes on the **first three frets**.

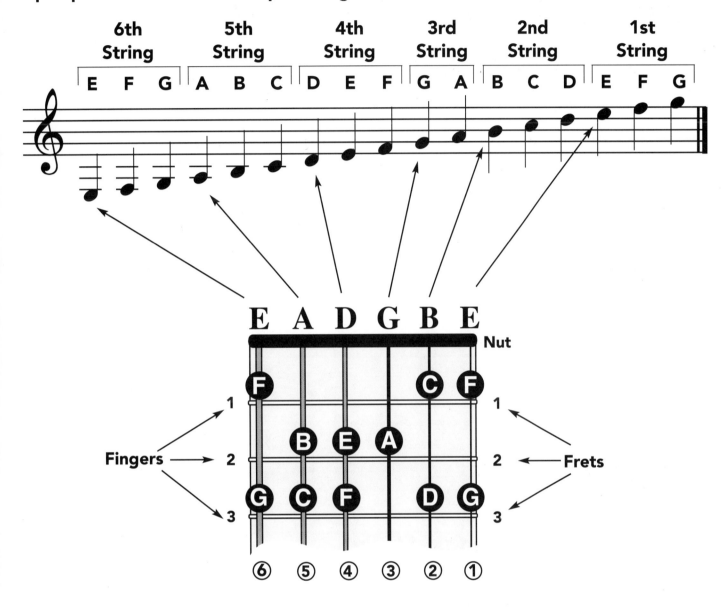

By playing through the notes you will notice **B** to **C** and **E** to **F** are only **one fret apart** (called a **semitone**), whereas all other notes are **two frets apart** (called a **tone**). The distance between notes of the musical alphabet can be set out as such:

A   B   C   D   E   F   G   A

semitone (i.e. one fret apart) - all others are tones (i.e. 2 frets apart)

It is essential for you to remember this pattern of notes.

CHECKLIST
- Revise all pieces and exercises so far studied.
- Double-check your timing and smoothness of sound. To do this, try recording yourself.
- Remember to watch the music, **not** the guitar.
- Can you comfortably read the **notation** at this stage?

LESSON SEVEN

CHORDS AND ARPEGGIOS
USING FREE STROKE

A **chord** consists of a combination of two or more notes played together (e.g. ).

An **arpeggio** is the playing of a chord in single note fashion (e.g. ♩ ♪ ♪).

PRELIMINARY STUDIES FOR SPANISH BALLAD

CD 1 **37.0**   **Chord Study**

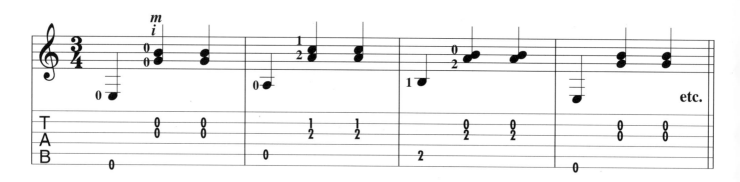

CD 1 **37.1**   **Arpeggio Study**

Arpeggio Variation

38. Spanish Ballad (Duet)

In this duet the top notes are to be played by the teacher.

39. Arpeggio Variation on the above

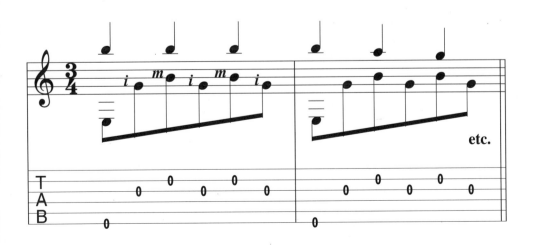

etc.

 **40.0**

Waltz with Variations
(using chords and arpeggios)

Carulli

 **40.1**   **Variation 1**

TAB to be written in by student.

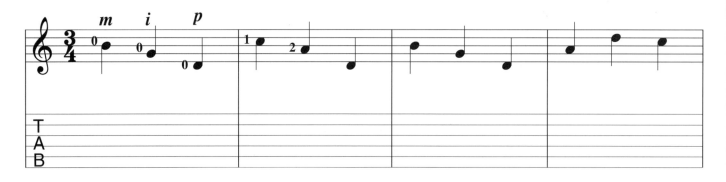

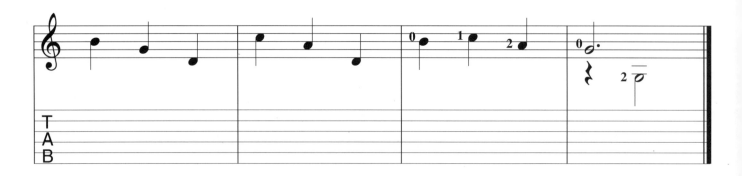

CD 1 40.2 Variation 2

Notation to be written in by student.

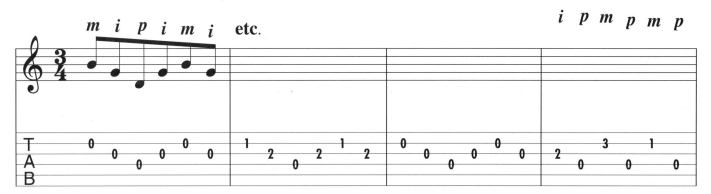

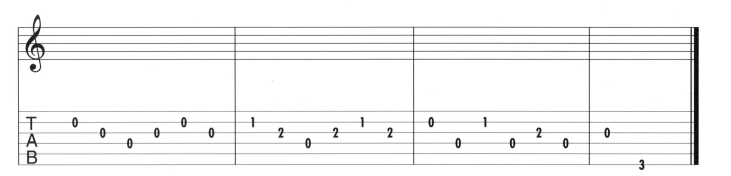

CD 1 41. Bolero (Duet)

Ravel

A full arrangement of **Bolero** is available in *Popular Classics of the Great Composers Vol.1* by Jason Waldron (LTP Publishing - visit **www.learntoplaymusic.com**).

Note: The student can now begin to use *Repertoire Book 1*, Part 5.

LESSON EIGHT

SHARPS

A **sharp** (♯) is a sign, placed immediately **before** a note, which **raises the pitch** (highness or lowness) **of that note** by **one semitone (one fret)**. When you see a note with a sharp sign in front of it, you should first think of where the normal note is located (in music this is called the **natural** note), and then sharpen it by placing your **next finger** on the **next fret** along. Here are some examples:

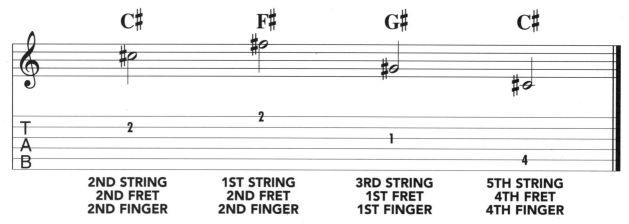

C♯	F♯	G♯	C♯
2ND STRING	1ST STRING	3RD STRING	5TH STRING
2ND FRET	2ND FRET	1ST FRET	4TH FRET
2ND FINGER	2ND FINGER	1ST FINGER	4TH FINGER

The use of the sharp sign introduces five new notes, occurring in between the seven natural notes which you already know. The following exercise outlines all twelve notes which occur within one octave of music. Play through it **very slowly**, and be sure to use correct fingering for the sharpened notes.

CD 1   42.0

You will notice that there is **no sharp** between **B** and **C**, or between **E** and **F**. The exercise you have just played is called a **chromatic scale**. It is referred to as the **A chromatic scale** because the starting and finishing notes are **A** (this is called the **key note** or **tonic**). The chromatic scale consists entirely of **semitones** i.e. it moves up (or down) one fret at a time.

CD 1   42.1   Here is the **G** chromatic scale:

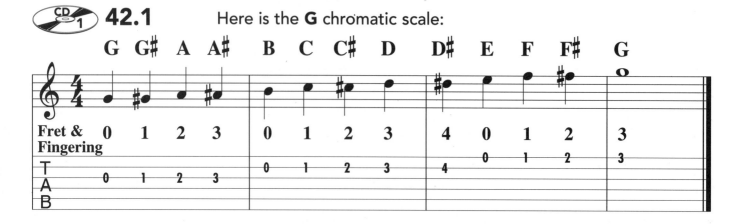

When a note is sharpened it **remains sharp** until either a **bar line** or a **natural sign** (♮) cancels it. Check the following notes:

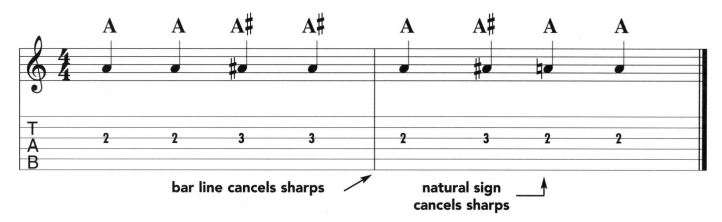

bar line cancels sharps ↗

natural sign ↑
cancels sharps

43. Arpeggio Study (using F♯ and D♯)

Carulli

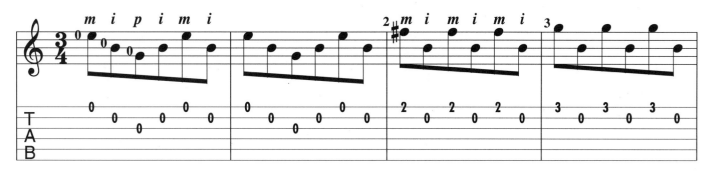

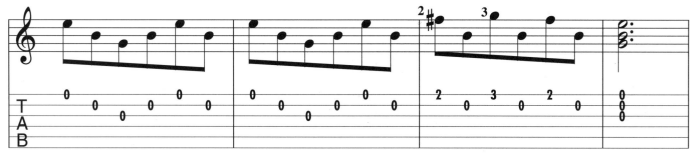

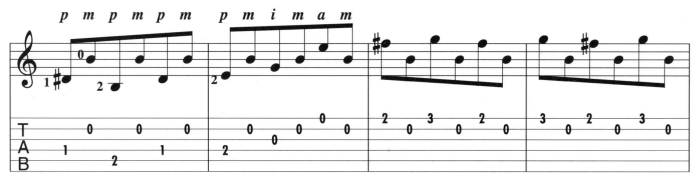

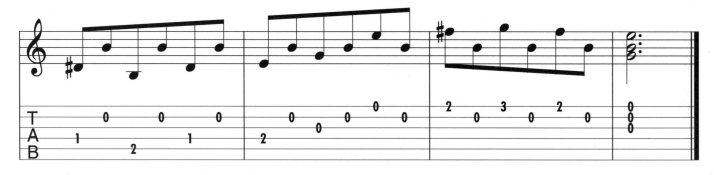

44. Malaguena

Be sure to alternate in scale passages using rest stroke, i.e. line 3.
Note the use of G♯s which only apply to the bar in which they occur unless indicated otherwise, i.e. line 3, bar 1.

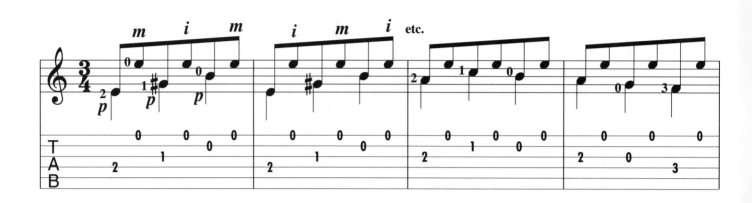

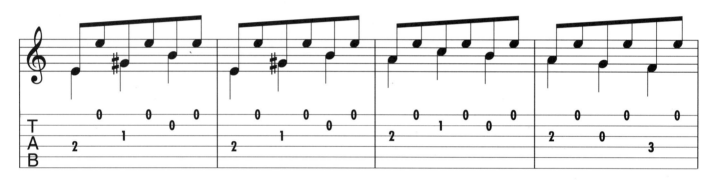

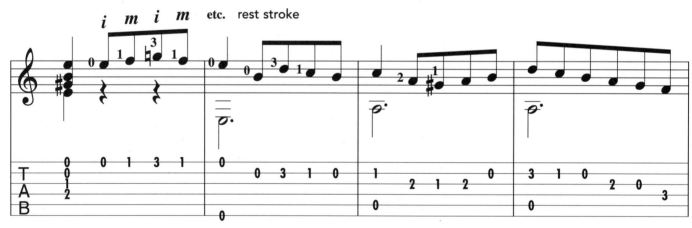

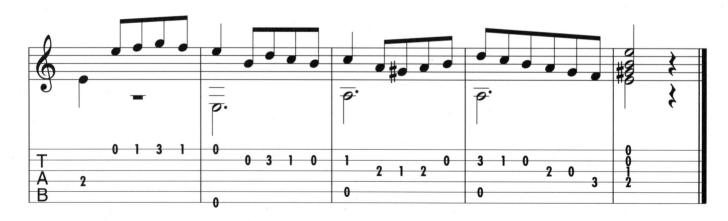

FLATS

A **flat** (♭) is a sign, placed immediately **before** a note, which **lowers the pitch of that note** by **one semitone**. Locate the following flats:

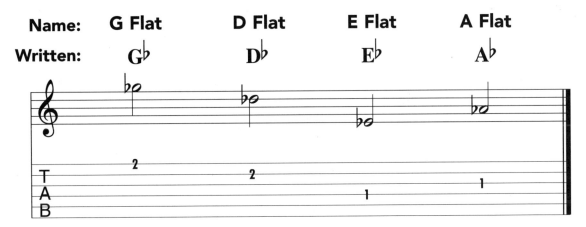

Name:	G Flat	D Flat	E Flat	A Flat
Written:	G♭	D♭	E♭	A♭

When an open string note is flattened, the new note must be located on the **next lower string** e.g.:

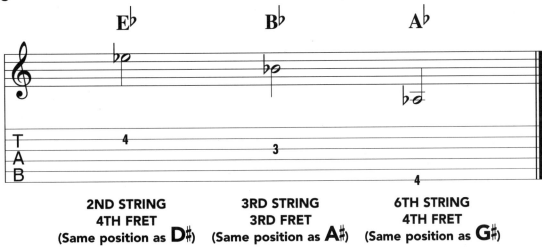

2ND STRING	3RD STRING	6TH STRING
4TH FRET	3RD FRET	4TH FRET
(Same position as D♯)	(Same position as A♯)	(Same position as G♯)

You will notice that it is possible for the same note (in pitch) to have two different names. For example, F♯ = G♭ and G♯ = A♭. These are referred to as **enharmonic** notes. The following fretboard diagram outlines all of the notes in the **first position** on the guitar (including both names for the enharmonic notes). The first position consists of the **open string notes** and the notes on the **first four frets**.

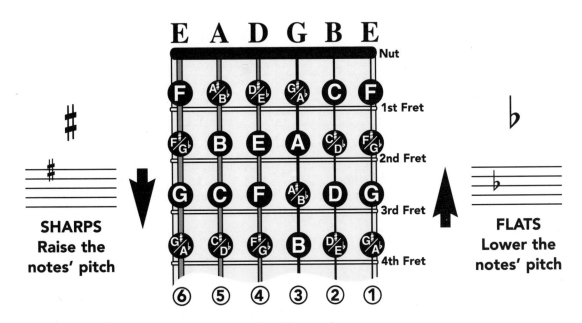

 **45.**

Here are two octaves of the **E chromatic scale**, ascending using sharps and descending using flats.

As with sharps, flats are cancelled by a bar line or by a natural sign.

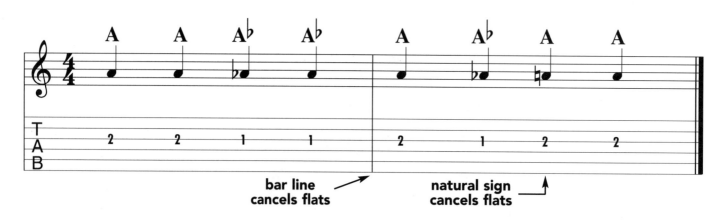

46. Hall of the Mountain King

Grieg

Be sure to observe the extensive use of ♯s and ♭s in this piece as well as the important left hand fingering.

Note: Also use of repeat signs and first and second time endings.

Note: Repeat signs will not always be observed in the CD recordings to follow.

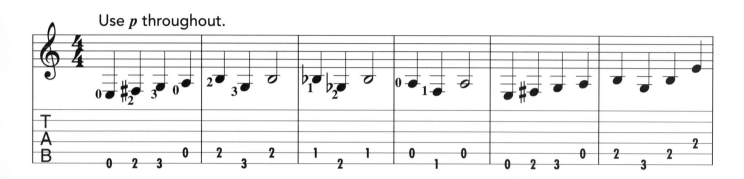

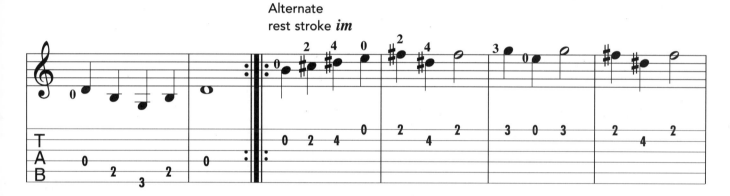

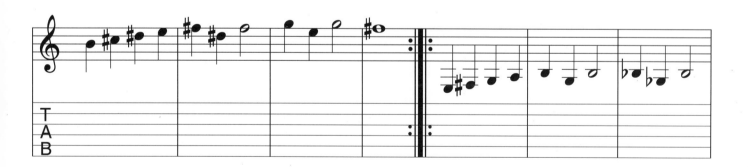

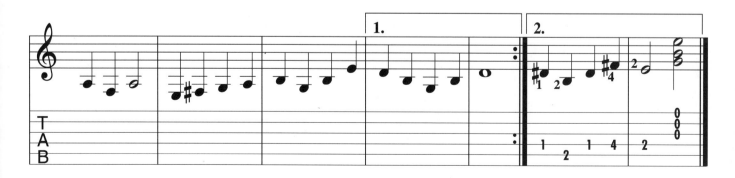

Note: See *Repertoire Book 1* Part 6 and onwards, for examples using ♯s, ♭s and ♮s.

SOUND PRODUCTION

By now, the student should be able to recognise the amazing degrees of tone variation which can be obtained by slightly changing the attack of the free and rest strokes, either by hand position or finger action. In general, a **flatter** nail stroke provides a brighter, sharper sound, whereas a more **side-on** nail stroke is rounder and more mellow. This great variety of tone (given exactly the same spot on the string), can be amplified immensely, as can be seen below.

TONE CONTRASTS ALONG THE STRING

Having established a consistent right hand position, it is now possible to experiment using the exercises and studies previously learned (along, of course, with those to come) by shifting the right hand (and arm) to achieve tone contrasts on different areas of the string. We can divide the string's plucking area into three tonal areas:

1. **Normal Position**: As seen below, this is the area most commonly used and can be considered rather neutral in tone.
2. **Ponticello** (or towards the bridge): It can be seen that the further the hand is shifted towards the bridge (from the normal position), the more metallic and harsh the sound becomes.
3. **Dolce** (mellow or sweet): conversely, the area towards the fingerboard becomes increasingly mellow and in direct contrast to ponticello.

Overall, it is most effective to use **ponticello** when playing passages in the lower positions, and **dolce** when playing in higher positions, as can be heard through experimentation.

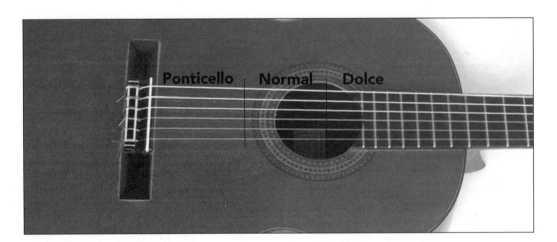

COMPOSITE NATURE OF THE GUITAR

We can think of the guitar as having similar characteristics to those of the piano (and harpsichord), i.e. the ability to create two or more simultaneous voices (called **polyphony** as introduced on page 37), albeit on a smaller scale, combined with the singing and tonal qualities of stringed instruments such as the violin and cello. Beethoven once described the guitar as a "miniature orchestra" because of its composite nature and myriad of sound possibilities. For this reason, the guitarist should always be experimenting to find the "**orchestral instrument**" best suited to describe any given musical passage.

LESSON NINE

SCALES AND KEY SIGNATURES
SCALES

A **scale** can be defined as a series of notes, in alphabetical order, going from any given note to its octave and based upon some form of set pattern. The pattern upon which most scales are based involves a set sequence of **tones** and/or **semitones**. On the guitar, a tone is two frets and a semitone is one fret. As an example, the B note is a tone higher than A (two frets), whereas the C note is only a semitone higher than B (one fret). Of the other natural notes in music, E and F are a semitone apart, and all the others are a tone apart.

Natural Notes: A   B   C   D   E   F   G   A

In music theory, a **tone** may be referred to as a **step** and a **semitone** as a **half - step**.

The three main types of scales that you need to become familiar with are the **chromatic** (see page 50), **major** and **minor scales**.

Scales should be memorized and practiced daily. Always play slowly and evenly at first, gradually building up speed.

Practice the scale using both rest stroke and free stroke. Use *im, ma, ia*.
Be sure to accommodate the right hand in its movement from the 1st string to the 6th string. You should raise or lower the forearm as seen in **photos A** and **B**. This adjustment allows the right hand fingers to remain in the correct shape for playing across the six strings without reaching or hooking.

photo A: Plucking ①

photo B: Plucking ⑥

Note: how the wrist is gathered more squarely to the bass strings for better sound quality and to avoid excessive scrapping on the wound strings by virtue of the angle of nail attack.

THE MAJOR SCALE

The most common scale in Western music is called the **major scale**. This scale is based upon a sequence of both tones and semitones, and is thus sometimes referred to as a **diatonic** scale. Here is the major scale sequence:

TONE	TONE	SEMITONE	TONE	TONE	TONE	SEMITONE
T	T	S	T	T	T	S

ONE OCTAVE, C MAJOR SCALE

Starting on the C note and following through this sequence gives the **C major scale**:

T=tone (2 fret)
S=semitone (1 fret)

Roman numerals are used to number each note of the major scale, Thus F is the 4th note (IV) of the C major scale, G is the 5th (V), and so on.
The major scale will always give the familiar sound of **do, re, mi, fa, so, la, ti, do**.

The major scale **always** uses the same sequence of tones and semitones, no matter what note is used as the tonic. All major scales are listed below.

		T		T		S		T		T		T		S	
C MAJOR*	C		D		E		F		G		A		B		C
G MAJOR*	G		A		B		C		D		E		F♯		G
D MAJOR*	D		E		F♯		G		A		B		C♯		D
A MAJOR*	A		B		C♯		D		E		F♯		G♯		A
E MAJOR*	E		F♯		G♯		A		B		C♯		D♯		E
B MAJOR	B		C♯		D♯		E		F♯		G♯		A♯		B
F♯ MAJOR	F♯		G♯		A♯		B		C♯		D♯		E♯		F♯
F MAJOR*	F		G		A		B♭		C		D		E		F
B♭ MAJOR*	B♭		C		D		E♭		F		G		A		B♭
E♭ MAJOR	E♭		F		G		A♭		B♭		C		D		E♭
A♭ MAJOR	A♭		B♭		C		D♭		E♭		F		G		A♭
D♭ MAJOR	D♭		E♭		F		G♭		A♭		B♭		C		D♭
G♭ MAJOR	G♭		A♭		B♭		C♭		D♭		E♭		F		G♭
Roman Numerals	I		II		III		IV		V		VI		VII		VIII

* Major keys and scales studied in this method.

If you look at the major scales in the chart on the previous page, you will notice, in order to maintain the correct sequence of tones and semitones, all major scales except C major involve the use of either sharps or flats. You will also notice, when playing these scales, that they all maintain the familiar sound of **do**, **re**, **mi**, **fa**, **so**, **la**, **ti**, **do**.

MINOR SCALES

In Western music there are **three different minor scales**. These are the **pure minor**, the **harmonic minor** and the **melodic minor**. Each features a slightly different sequence of tones and semitones, as illustrated in the examples below using **A** as the tonic.

A MINOR, PURE SCALE

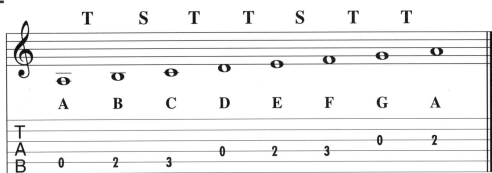

A MINOR, HARMONIC - VII note sharpened (called the LEADING NOTE)

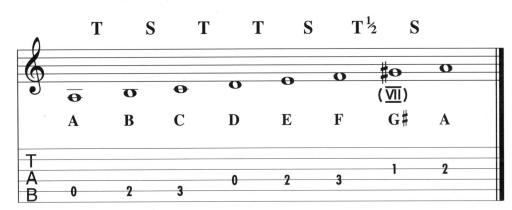

ONE OCTAVE, A MELODIC MINOR SCALE - VI and VII notes sharpened when ascending and returned to natural when descending.

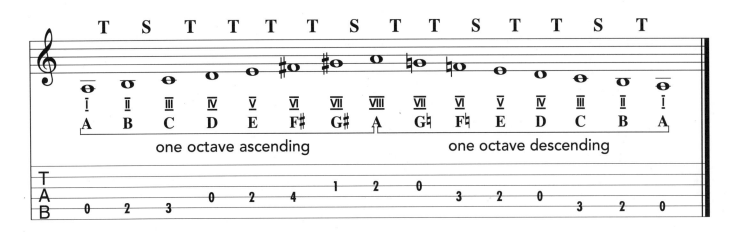

Of the three minor scales outlined on the previous page, the **melodic minor** is the most commonly used. All minor scales are listed on the chart below

MELODIC MINOR SCALES IN ALL KEYS

Interval pattern (ascending/descending): T S T T T S T T S T T S T

	I	II	III	IV	V	VI	VII	VIII	VII	VI	V	IV	III	II	I
A MELODIC MINOR*	A	B	C	D	E	F#	G#	A	G♮	F♮	E	D	C	B	A
E MELODIC MINOR*	E	F#	G	A	B	C#	D#	E	D♮	C♮	B	A	G	F#	E
B MELODIC MINOR*	B	C#	D	E	F#	G#	A#	B	A♮	G♮	F#	E	D	C#	B
F# MELODIC MINOR*	F#	G#	A	B	C#	D#	E#	F#	E♮	D♮	C#	B	A	G#	F#
C# MELODIC MINOR*	C#	D#	E	F#	G#	A#	B#	C#	B♮	A♮	G#	F#	E	D#	C#
G# MELODIC MINOR	G#	A#	B	C#	D#	E#	G	G#	F#	E♮	D#	C#	B	A#	G#
D# MELODIC MINOR	D#	E#	F#	G#	A#	B#	D	D#	C#	B♮	A#	G#	F#	E#	D#
D MELODIC MINOR*	D	E	F	G	A	B♮	C#	D	C♮	B♭	A	G	F	E	D
G MELODIC MINOR*	G	A	B♭	C	D	E♮	F#	G	F	E♭	D	C	B♭	A	G
C MELODIC MINOR	C	D	E♭	F	G	A♮	B♮	C	B♭	A♭	G	F	E♭	D	C
F MELODIC MINOR	F	G	A♭	B♭	C	D♮	E♮	F	E♭	D♭	C	B♭	A♭	G	F
B♭ MELODIC MINOR	B♭	C	D♭	E♭	F	G♮	A♮	B	A♭	G♭	F	E♭	D♭	C	B♭
E♭ MELODIC MINOR	E♭	F	G♭	A♭	B♭	C♮	D♮	E♭	D♭	C♭	B♭	A♭	G♭	F♭	E♭
ROMAN NUMERALS	I	II	III	IV	V	VI	VII	VIII	VII	VI	V	IV	III	II	I

* Minor keys and scales studied in this book.

KEYS AND KEY SIGNATURES

When music is talked of as being in a particular key, it means that the melody is based upon the major/or minor scale with the same name e.g. in the key of C, C major scale notes (i.e. C, D, E, F, G, A and B) will occur much more frequently than notes that do not belong to the C scale (i.e. sharpened and flattened notes).

In the key of G, G scale notes will be most common (i.e. the notes G, A, B, C, D, E and F# will occur frequently). You will notice here a sharp sign is placed on the F line (the top one) of the staff at the beginning of each line. This is referred to as the **key signature**: thus the key signature of G major is F♯ .

Below are the key signatures for all keys. Each key signature applies to one major key and one minor key. These are called **relative keys** and are discussed on the following page.

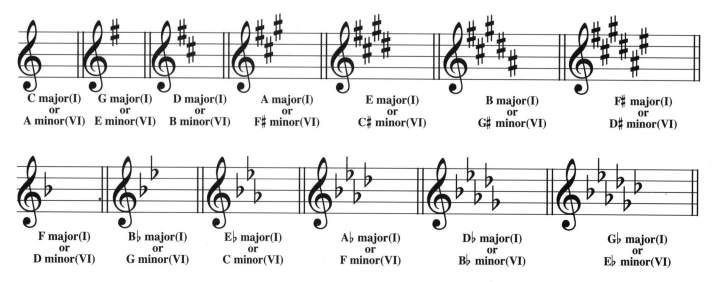

C major(I) or A minor(VI) G major(I) or E minor(VI) D major(I) or B minor(VI) A major(I) or F# minor(VI) E major(I) or C# minor(VI) B major(I) or G# minor(VI) F# major(I) or D# minor(VI)

F major(I) or D minor(VI) B♭ major(I) or G minor(VI) E♭ major(I) or C minor(VI) A♭ major(I) or F minor(VI) D♭ major(I) or B♭ minor(VI) G♭ major(I) or E♭ minor(VI)

It can be seen, then, that each key signature is a shorthand representation of the scale, showing only the sharps or flats which occur in that scale. Where an additional sharp or flat occurs, it is not included as part of the key signature, but is written in the music, e.g. in the **key of G**, if a **D♯** note occurs, the sharp sign will be written immediately before the **D** note, **not** at the beginning of the line as part of the key signature. These notes are called **accidentals**.

RELATIVE KEYS

if you compare the **A natural minor** scale with the **C major** scale you will notice that they contain the same notes (except starting on a different note). Because of this, these two scales are referred to as "relatives"; **A minor** is the relative minor of **C major** and vice versa.

Major Scale: C Major

Relative Minor Scale: A Natural Minor

The harmonic and melodic minor scale variations are also relatives of the same major scale, e.g. **A harmonic** and **A melodic minor** are relatives of **C major**.

For every major scale (and ever major chord) there is a relative minor scale which is based upon the **6th note** of the major scale. This is outlined in the table below.

MAJOR KEY (I)	C	D♭	D	E♭	E	F	F♯	G♭	G	A♭	A	B♭	B
RELATIVE MINOR KEY (VI)	Am	B♭m	Bm	Cm	C♯m	Dm	D♯m	E♭m	Em	Fm	F♯m	Gm	G♯m

To determine whether a piece is in a major key or the relative minor key, look at the last note or chord of the piece. A piece will often finish on the root note or the root chord which indicates the key. E.g., if the key signature contained one sharp, and the last chord of the piece was **Em**, the key would probably be **E minor**, not **G major**. Minor key signatures are always based on the natural minor scale. The sharpened 6th and 7th degrees from the harmonic and melodic minor scales are not indicated in the key signature. This usually means there are accidentals (temporary sharps, flats or naturals) in melodies created from these scales.

LESSON TEN

MAJOR AND MINOR KEYS

KEY OF C MAJOR

C MAJOR SCALE *(no sharps or flats in key signature)*

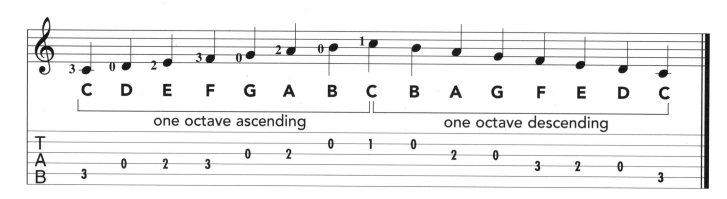

CHORDS

A chord is a group of 2, 3 or more notes played simultaneously. Different types of chords can be formed by using different combinations of notes. The most basic type of chord contains three different notes and is called a **triad**. The most common triad is the **major chord**. All major chords contain three notes taken from the major scale of the same letter name. These three notes are the $\bar{\text{I}}$ (first), $\overline{\text{III}}$ (third) and $\bar{\text{V}}$ (fifth) degrees of the major scale, so the **chord formula** for the major chord is:

Notes in Chord

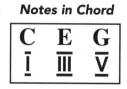

The C Major Chord

The C major chord is constructed from the C major scale. Using the above chord formula on the C major scale below, it can be seen that the C major chord contains the notes **C**, **E** and **G**.

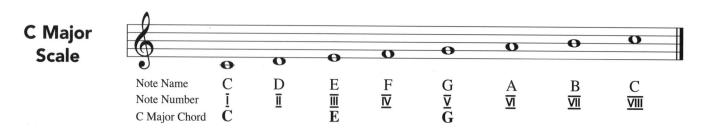

Once you have the correct notes for a C chord they can be arranged in any order. As long as the notes are still C, E and G, you still have a C chord. For example a C chord could be played C E G, or E G C, or G C E, or even G E C. These various arrangements of the notes within a chord are called **inversions**. It is also possible to **double** notes within a chord. For example the diagram below shows a common way of playing the C major chord on the guitar. It contains two C notes and two E notes. It is still a C major chord because it only contains notes called C, E and G. Doubling notes is common when playing chords on the guitar.

C CHORD FINGERING

DOUBLE C AND E NOTES

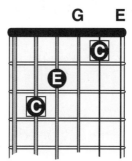

CHORD SYMBOLS

Chords are indicated by a chord symbol above the music notation (see below). In the case of major chords, the symbol consists only of the letter name of the chord. E.g. a C chord is indicated by the letter C, an A chord is indicated by the letter A, a B♭ chord is indicated by the letter B♭, etc. Minor chords are indicated by the letter followed by **m**.

CHORDS IN THE KEY OF C MAJOR

Every major and minor key contains **three principle chords** derived from the scale.
1. the **TONIC (I)**: first note of the scale
2. the **SUB-DOMINANT (IV)**: fourth note of the scale
3. the **DOMINANT SEVENTH (V7)**: fifth note of the scale (see following page "Dominant 7th chords")

The most common sequence of these three chords is from **tonic** to **sub-dominant** to **dominant 7th** and back to **tonic**. In the key of C major, C Ī is the tonic, F ĪV is the sub-dominant and G7 V̄7 is the dominant 7th. Thus the basic chord sequence is: C - F - G7 - C, as illustrated below:

 **47.**

CHORD VOICINGS

As with all chords, there is more than one fingering on the guitar for a C chord. The adjacent diagram shows an alternative voicing for C. The term **voicing** means the arrangement of notes in a particular fingering, with the notes arranged from the lowest to the highest. The C chord will always contain C ($\underline{I}$), E ($\underline{III}$) and G ($\underline{V}$), but it is possible to arrange these notes in any order. The fingering shown here is voiced $\underline{III}$, $\underline{V}$, $\underline{I}$, $\underline{V}$.

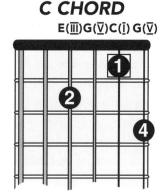

C CHORD

E($\underline{III}$)G($\underline{V}$)C($\underline{I}$)G($\underline{V}$)

DOMINANT 7TH CHORDS

Like the major chord, 7th chords can be derived from the major scale. A 7th chord is obtained by adding the flattened 7th note of the scale to a major chord.

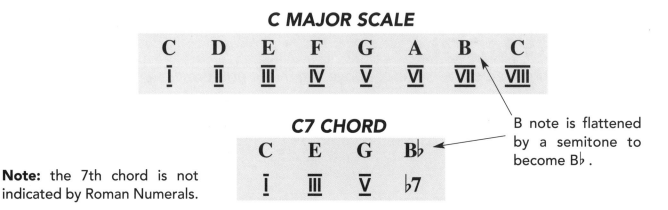

C MAJOR SCALE

C	D	E	F	G	A	B	C
$\underline{I}$	$\underline{II}$	$\underline{III}$	$\underline{IV}$	$\underline{V}$	$\underline{VI}$	$\underline{VII}$	$\underline{VIII}$

C7 CHORD

C	E	G	B♭
$\underline{I}$	$\underline{III}$	$\underline{V}$	♭7

B note is flattened by a semitone to become B♭.

Note: the 7th chord is not indicated by Roman Numerals.

Because the notes of a dominant 7th chord are the first ($\underline{I}$), third ($\underline{III}$), fifth ($\underline{V}$) and flattened seventh (♭7) notes of the major scale, the chord formula for the seventh chord is: $\underline{I}$ $\underline{III}$ $\underline{V}$ ♭7

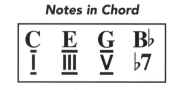

Notes in Chord

C	E	G	B♭
$\underline{I}$	$\underline{III}$	$\underline{V}$	♭7

CHORDS $\underline{I}$ $\underline{IV}$ AND $\underline{V}$ IN ALL KEYS

Shown below is a table of chords $\underline{I}$, $\underline{IV}$ and $\underline{V}$ in all twelve keys used in music, major and minor. In any key, chord $\underline{V}$ can be either a major chord or a dominant 7th chord.

KEY	$\underline{I}$	$\underline{IV}$	$\underline{V}$
C	C	F	G
G	G	C	D
D	D	G	A
A	A	D	E
E	E	A	B
B	B	E	F#
F#	F#	B	C#
F	F	B♭	C
B♭	B♭	E♭	F
E♭	E♭	A♭	B♭
A♭	A♭	D♭	E♭
D♭	D♭	G♭	A♭
G♭	G♭	C♭	D♭

KEY	$\underline{I}$	$\underline{IV}$	$\underline{V}$
Am	Am	Dm	E
Em	Em	Am	B
Bm	Bm	Em	F#
F#m	F#m	Bm	C#
C#m	C#m	F#m	G#
G#m	G#m	C#m	D#
D#m	D#m	G#m	A#
Dm	Dm	Gm	A
Gm	Gm	Cm	D
Cm	Cm	Fm	G
Fm	Fm	B♭m	C
B♭m	B♭m	E♭m	F
A♭m	A♭m	D♭m	E♭

Note: minor chords are indicated as **m**

TECHNICAL COMMON DENOMINATORS

Most pieces of music are written in set musical and technical patterns, and from these patterns we can extract exercises and studies to be practiced as separate entities. For instance, the **Waltz** on page 66 is essentially using just two chords, tonic C and dom.7 G7 (shown above notation) and groups of right hand arpeggios. These elements which occur repeatedly can be considered **common denominators**, and should be practiced separately before attempting to put the piece together. Note that the G7 is not exactly as presented on page 63, but uses the notes essential to this chord (see page 64 "Chord Voicing") which, regardless of their pitch (highness or lowness) used together can only constitute a G7 chord.

Firstly practice the left hand changes as **block chords** (all notes played together) by repeating the C, G7, C etc., until it can be achieved with little problem (see **Ex.1**).

Next , practice the right hand arpeggios separately using C or G7, or open strings (as seen in **Ex.2**).

By concentrating on each hand individually, it will make it easier to combine both hands as written, because each will be working almost automatically.
This practice method should be used at all levels of playing.

CD 1 48.0

Ex.1   **Ex.2**

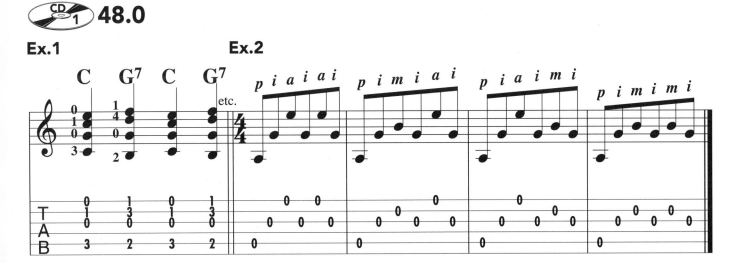

COLLECTING GUITAR MUSIC

It is very important for the student to continually be adding to his or her guitar music collection for both sight reading and technical development. There are many comprehensive albums of guitar music and arrangements readily available from stores or via mail order featuring important studies and pieces by composers from the Classical, Baroque, Renaissance, Romantic and Modern periods. The student should not be afraid to purchase and attempt music of a higher standard that they may have heard through recordings etc., as it can sometimes be beneficial to push limitations in favour of inspiration.

MUSICAL FORM

Form refers to the pattern (or plan) of individual sections of music within a piece. The most common section lengths are 4 or 8 bars. One of the most common types of form is called **BINARY FORM**, where the order of the sections is [A] [B] . Sometimes these sections are repeated (as in the following **waltz**) and, whilst the two sections do not have to be identical, they must retain similar characteristics.

48.1 Waltz

Carulli

This is an excellent and simple right hand arpeggio study in C major. Play strongly and evenly, remembering to observe the time value of the dotted half notes by holding them for the entire bar.

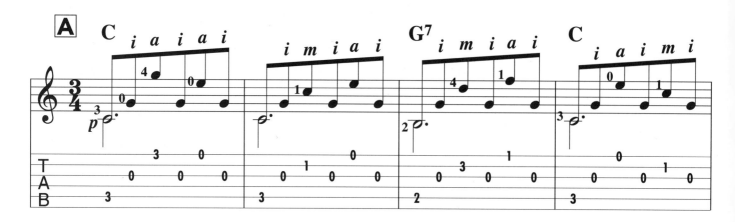

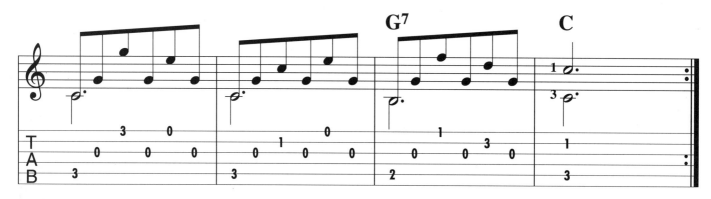

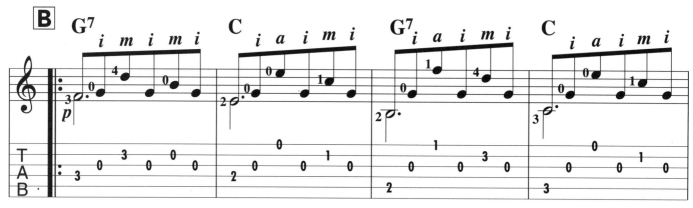

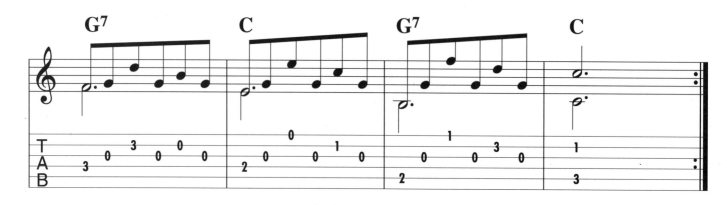

RIGHT HAND TECHNIQUE REVIEW

Re-examining rest stroke and free stroke gripping action.

Having had considerable experience with both rest and free stroke, it is a good time for the student to re-appraise one of the most important and intricate techniques, that being right hand finger action and gripping or placement between flesh and nail for both strokes.

It can be observed that both strokes are essentially the same for **1**, **2** and **3** and the only major difference occurs at **4**. Also that the string is set in motion by the **nail only** after having used the junction of the flesh and nail as a reference point.

REST STROKE

With the right hand correctly positioned :
1. Prepare finger as shown below.
2. Bring finger to the string and lightly "jam" in the groove between the flesh and nail.
3. Allow the tip joint to collapse till the finger is virtually straight from middle joint to tip.
4. This collapsing of the tip joint should allow the finger to easily pluck the string with the **nail only** coming to rest on the adjacent string.

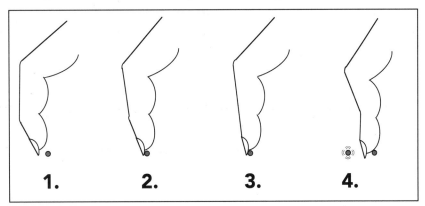

FREE STROKE

1. As rest stroke.
2. As rest stroke.
3. As rest stroke.
4. Having collapsed the tip joint, the finger will easily execute the pluck and stop as seen below slightly curved inwards before relaxing back to **1.**

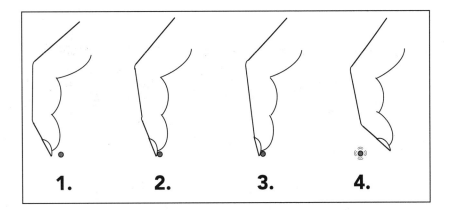

It will be found that by allowing the finger to relax, it will return to **1.** ready to pluck again. Obviously, the degree of "string grip" when playing single notes, chords or alternating is dependent upon the speed required or musical taste (refer "Legato and Staccato" pg. 169).

TRIPLETS

A **triplet** is a group of three notes played in the same time as two notes of the same kind. In the following study, **eighth note triplets** are introduced, which are indicated thus: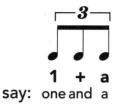

These eighth note triplets are played in the same time as two eighth notes (i.e. 1 beat), and are counted as such:

say: one and a

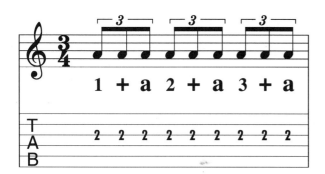

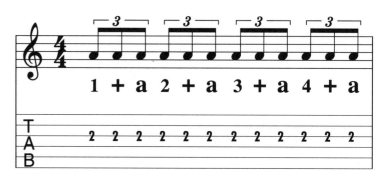

It can be seen from these examples above that each note is worth ⅓ **of a beat**.

The triplet indication, ⌐**3**⌐ , can be written either above or below the note group.

49. Study in C

This piece can sound very effective by repeating each bar.
Note: common denominators, *pim*, *pma*

SIXTEENTH NOTES

The following piece introduces the **sixteenth note**  (**sixteenth note rest**) which is worth a **quarter of a beat**. Four sixteenth notes equal one quarter note:

e.g. (figure showing four sixteenth notes = one quarter note)

Sixteenth notes are counted by using syllables 'e-and-a' after the beat count:

Count: 1 e + a 2 e + a 3 e + a 4 e + a

Count out loud as you play the following example (slowly) and notice the different sound for each part of the beat – **one ee and ah, two ee and ah...** etc (written **1 e + a, 2 e + a...** etc).

(musical staff example)

Count   **1 e + a 2 e + a 3 e + a 4 e + a**

DOTTED EIGHTH NOTES

The next piece also introduces the **dotted eighth note** which is worth ¾ of a beat. It has the same time value as an eighth note tied to a sixteenth note.

Count: 1 a 2 a

 50. **Air (from Water Music)** using dotted eighth notes   Handel

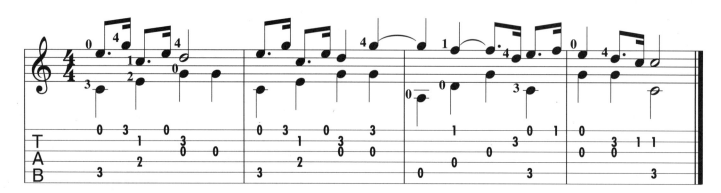

A full arrangement of the **Air** is available in **Popular Classics of the Great Composers Vol. 6** by Jason Waldron (LTP Publishing - visit **www.learntoplaymusic.com**).

51. Study in C

Carulli

This study combines the use of chords, arpeggios and single notes. Be sure to maintain a consistent tone and volume throughout. You will notice that the stems of the bass notes (played by *p*) point both downward and upward, e.g. bar two. This is a common technique of writing guitar music, to help distinguish the bass line and yet maintain the appearance of an arpeggio.

Note: see *Repertoire Book 1*, Part 7 for more pieces in the key of C.

LESSON ELEVEN

KEY OF A MINOR

A MELODIC MINOR SCALE (see page 59)
(relative minor to C, no sharps or flats in the key signature)

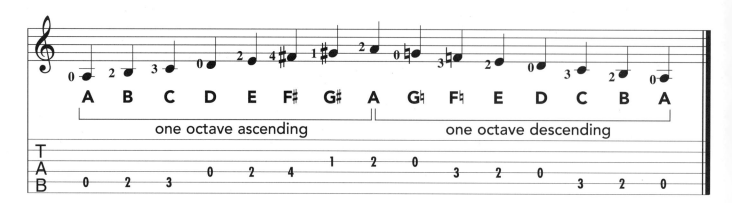

A	B	C	D	E	F♯	G♯	A	G♮	F♮	E	D	C	B	A

one octave ascending   one octave descending

The following arpeggio example introduces **⁶⁄₈ time** where there are **six eighth notes per bar**.

Note: minor chords indicated as **m**

Count: 1 2 3 4 5 6

 **52.**

CHORDS   **ARPEGGIO**

Tonic sub.dom dom7 Tonic
Am   **Dm**   **E7**   **Am**

Count: 1 2 3 4 5 6

Note: In the following **Study in A minor** (page 73) the use of the E chord $\left(\frac{E}{I}, \frac{G\#}{III}, \frac{B}{V}\right)$ where no flattened 7th (D natural) is used to create the E7 chord (see page 64).

It also introduces the **sixteenth note Rest** (𝄿).

53. Study in A Minor

Giuliani

Note: right hand common denominators, *pimiaimi, pipi, pima,* chord symbols and the use of sixteenth notes and rests.

sixteenth note rest

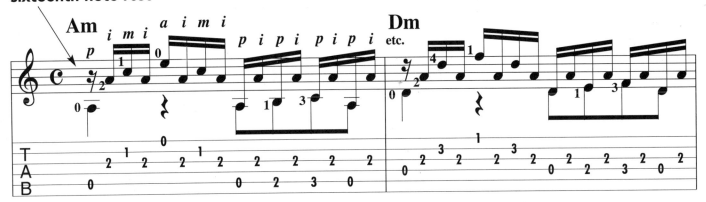

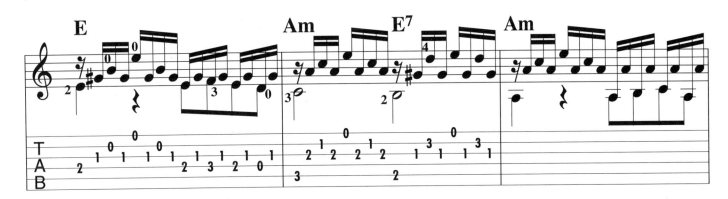

DOTTED QUARTER NOTE RHYTHMS

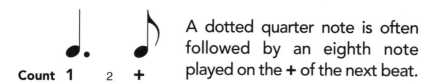

Count 1 2 +

A dotted quarter note is often followed by an eighth note played on the + of the next beat.

Count out loud as you play the following example. You will need to have control of this rhythm to play the next piece, **Greensleeves**.

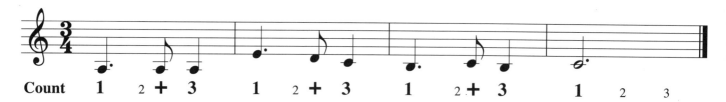

Count 1 2 + 3 1 2 + 3 1 2 + 3 1 2 3

54. Greensleeves

Anon.

Notice how the melody of **Greensleeves** moves from the bass (lower) to the treble (higher) and back to the bass several times throughout. Take particular notice of the ties and **dotted quarter notes**.

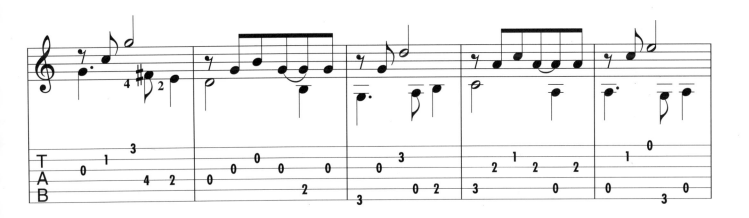

(treble)

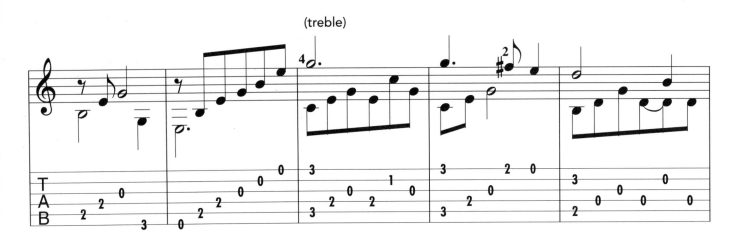

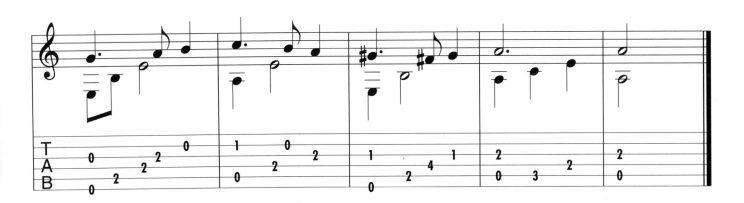

Note: the student can now begin to use **Repertoire Book 1**, Parts 8 and 9.

LESSON TWELVE

KEY OF G MAJOR
G SCALE (one sharp, F♯ in key signature)

CD 1 55.

CHORDS   **ARPEGGIO**

Tonic sub.dom dom7 Tonic
G   **C**   **D7**   **G**

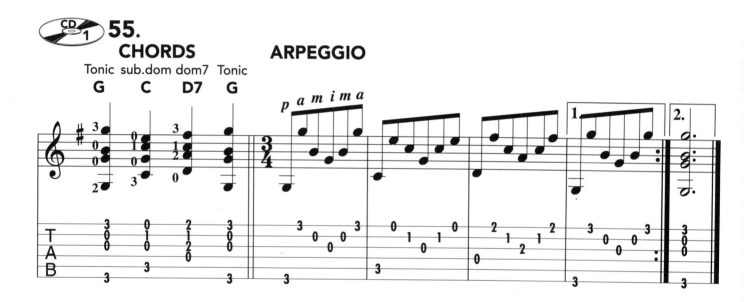

CD 1 56. Waltz in G

Sor

This **waltz** introduces ⅜ **time**, which is **three eighth note beats per bar**. ⅜ has the same waltz feel as ¾.

Count: 3   1 2 3   1 2 + 3

57. Study in G

Sor

Be sure to give full value to the whole notes by leaving the left hand fingers on the strings until the end of each bar. Carefully observe the **accidentals** (sharps, flats and naturals, not included in the key signature – see page 61) and follow the fingerings where marked. Alternate right hand fingers.

Note: the student can now begin to use **Repertoire Book 1**, Part 10.

KEY OF E MINOR

E MELODIC MINOR SCALE
(relative minor to G, one sharp, F# in key signature)

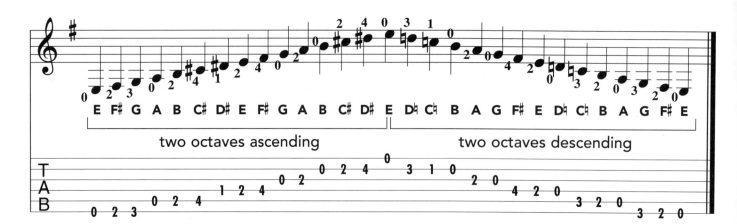

two octaves ascending   two octaves descending

 **58.**

CHORDS   ARPEGGIO

Tonic sub.dom dom7 Tonic
Em   Am   B7   Em

VARIATION

DETERMINING THE KEY OF A PIECE

It is important for you to be able to recognise what key a piece is in and the way to do this is to identify it from the sharps or flats of the key signature. The key signature, however, does not distinguish between major and relative minor keys; for example, a key signature of F sharp, (as in the previous page) could indicate **either** G major **or** E minor. The two main guidelines for determining whether a piece is in the major or relative minor key are:

1. The presence of the 7th note of the minor scale (the leading note). This is the only note of a minor scale (except the 'pure' minor) which is not found in its relative major, thus a D♯ note in the music will strongly suggest the key of E minor rather than G major.
2. The name of the finishing note (or chord). A piece very often finishes on its root note and thus an E note at the end would suggest the key of E minor (quite often a piece will also begin on the root note).

59. Sakura

Anon. (Japan)

In the following piece **D.C. al Fine** means to **return to the beginning** (**D.C.** stands for **Da Capo**, which means "the head") and play through to **Fine** (finish). Note how the study changes key from Em - G - Em. The process of a key change within a piece is called **modulation**.

Note: *D.C. al Fine* indication can be placed above or below line.

60. Study in Em and G

Carulli

Note: the student can now begin to use **Repertoire Book 1**, Part 11.

SECTION 2

THE FULL BAR AND THE HALF BAR

Often it becomes necessary to hold down more than one string and as many as six, and this is achieved by the use of the **full Bar** and **half Bar**. As demonstrated in the following photos, the **entire first finger** (1) is used to form the **full Bar** which covers all **six strings**, whilst only the **tip segment of the first finger** is used to cover any **combination of three adjacent strings**, in this case ③ ② and ① to form the **half Bar**. Make sure to keep the first finger **perfectly straight**, and **close to the fret** whilst executing the full Bar, in order to produce clear notes on each string without buzzing. Carefully study the photos of the half Bar as the angles and curves need to be correct, in particular the almost **pyramid** structure of the **middle joint** in **photo D**. Be sure to retain a chromatic left hand position and avoid bunching fingers during the use of the full and half Bars.

Note that the wrist is pushed out by the use of the full Bar (**photo A** and **C**) and that the thumb drops closer to the treble side of the fretboard.

- The **full Bar** is notated as **B**.
- The **half Bar** is notated as ½ **B**.
- The **B** and ½ **B** indication are then followed by a number which specifies the fret position.
  For example:

B3 means to use the **full Bar** across the **third fret**.
½ **B5** means to use the **half Bar** across the **fifth fret**.

photo A

photo B

photo C

photo D

KEY OF F MAJOR

F MAJOR SCALE (one flat, B♭ in key signature)

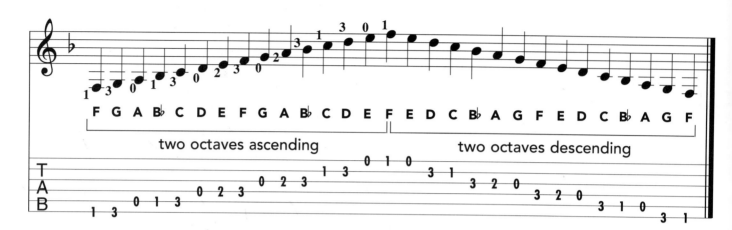

61.

Use the **full Bar** for F and B♭ chords. Remember to adjust the wrist as previously explained for the Bar and position normally for the C7.

62. Prelude in F

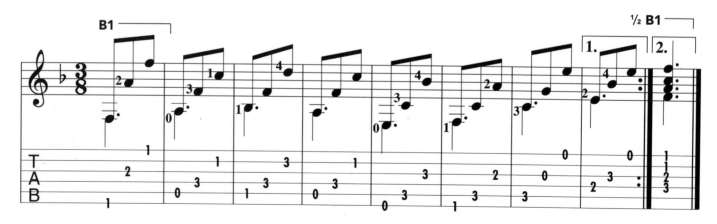

Note: see page 197 for more about the F chord Bar.

Use the **full Bar** throughout the next study. In order to play the open E, lift the Bar slightly whilst retaining a straight finger and leaving the tip segment lightly placed on the 6th string F. This technique is referred to as a **hinge Bar**.

CD 1 **63.** **Full Bar Study in F** Carulli

PIVOT FINGER

The following study introduces the **pivot finger** which remains in position on a note whilst other fingers move (see dotted indication). It is a very important technique, making pieces easier to play and helps to develop finger independence.

CD 1 **64.** **Half Bar Study in F** Carcassi

65. Duet in F

Carulli

Note: fingerings are deliberately omitted in order for the student to work out from the fingering provided on pages 82 and 83.

KEY OF D MINOR
D MELODIC MINOR SCALE
(relative minor to F, one flat, B♭ in key signature)

CHORDS   **ARPEGGIO**

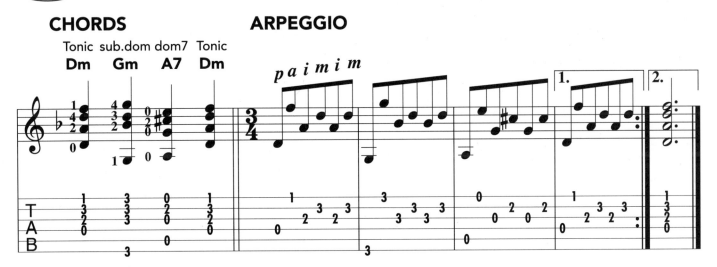

66.1   Minuet (18th Century Dance)   Purcell

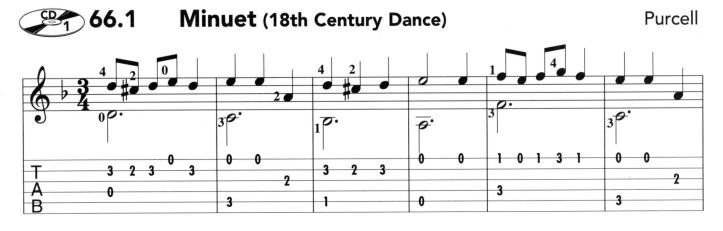

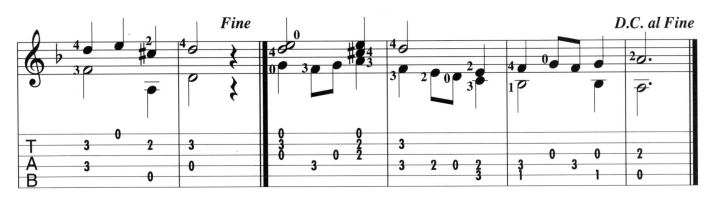

67. Study in Dm

Carulli

Note: extensive use of pivot fingers.

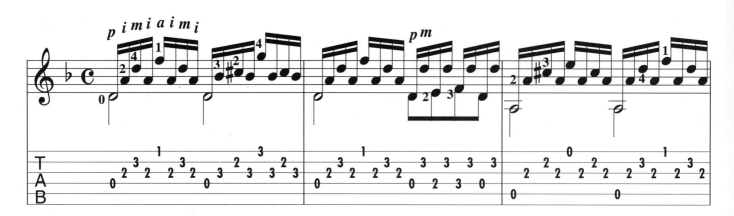

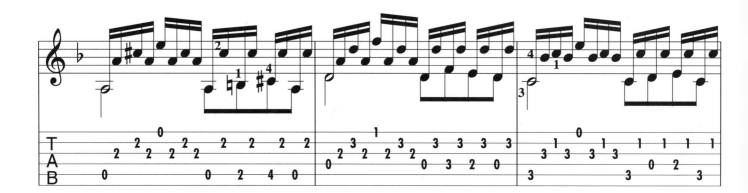

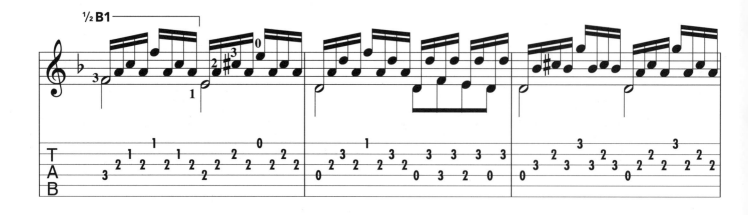

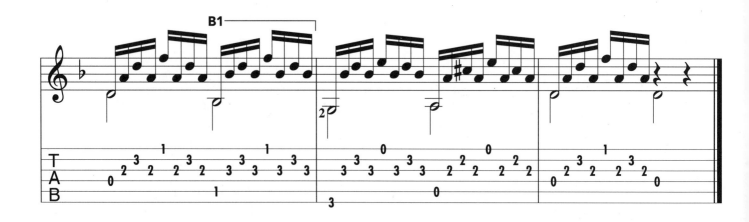

INTRODUCTION TO HARMONY

INTERVALS

The following section is intended to introduce the student to basic **harmony** (defined as any simultaneous combination of sounds) via the recognition of common **intervals**.
An interval is defined as the distance between two musical notes, (or degrees of a scale). Intervals are measured from the lower note upwards to the higher note.
Number and type names of intervals are used, i.e. a 3rd can be major or minor, depending upon the distance from one note to the next.

INTERVALS OF THE C MAJOR SCALE

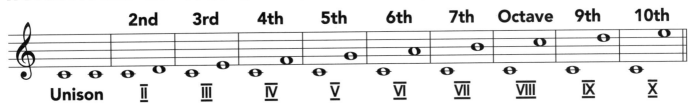

INTERVAL TYPES

There are five basic types of intervals which are listed below.

- **Perfect**
- **Major**
- **Minor**
- **Augmented**
- **Diminished**

Perfect intervals are 4ths, 5ths and octaves. If you widen any of these intervals by a semitone they become **augmented** and if you narrow them by a semitone they become **diminished**. **Major** intervals become **minor** if narrowed by a semitone and minor intervals become **major** if widened by a semitone. Examples of intervals which can be major or minor are 2nds, 3rds, 6ths and 7ths. An **augmented** interval can be created by widening a perfect or major interval by a semitone. A **diminished** interval can be created by narrowing a perfect or minor interval by a semitone.

For the purpose of demonstration, the difference between a major and minor 3rd is described below.

MAJOR 3RD INTERVALS (2 TONES APART)

MINOR 3RD INTERVALS (1½ TONES APART)

To change to a minor 3rd, lower the upper notes of the above intervals by one half tone (the minor 3rd is half a tone less than the major 3rd).

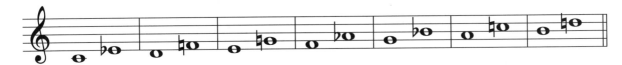

INTERVALS
THE OCTAVE

This interval covers the eight notes of the diatonic scale, i.e. C-C, D-D etc.

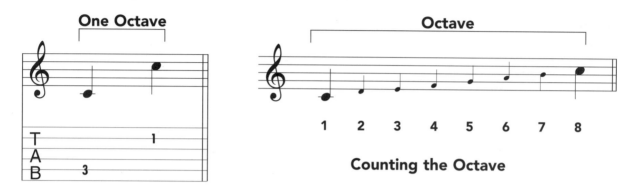

Counting the Octave

68. **Study in C (Octaves)** Aguado

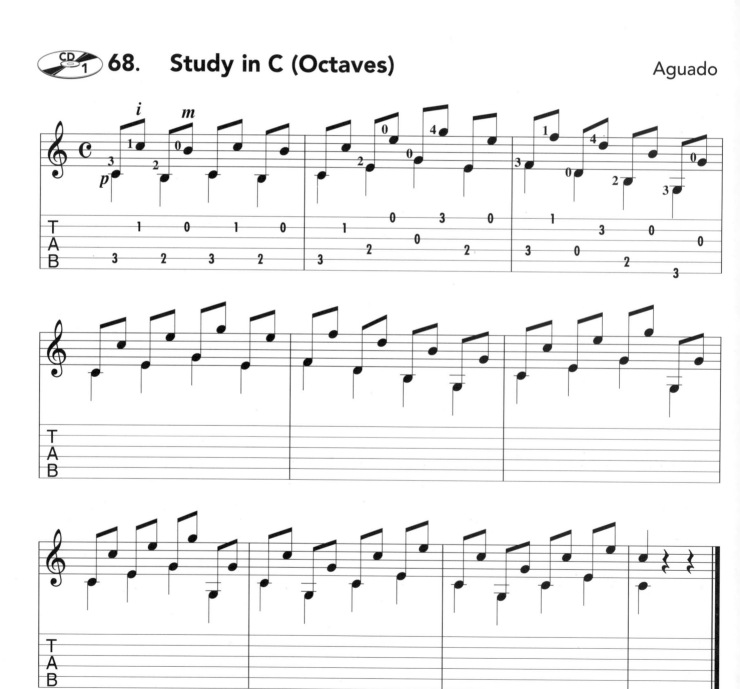

Note: Where omitted, TAB can be written in by student.

THE THIRD

This interval uses three degrees of the diatonic scale. The third determines the difference between a major and a minor scale and is easily identifiable as the notes sit on top of each other either on the lines or spaces.

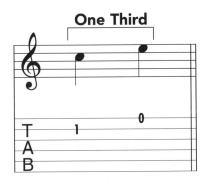

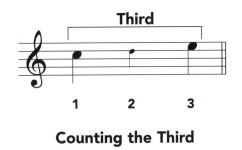

Counting the Third

 69. Study in A minor (3rds) Aguado

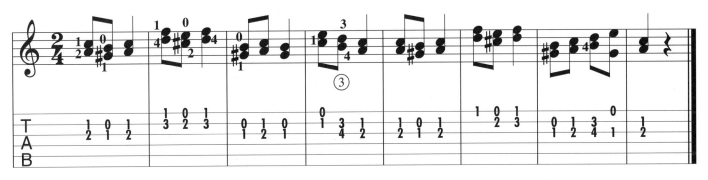

THE SIXTH

This interval uses six degrees of the diatonic scale.

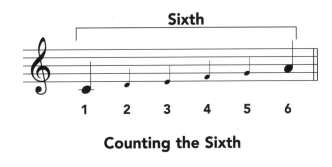

Counting the Sixth

 70. Study in C (6ths) Sor

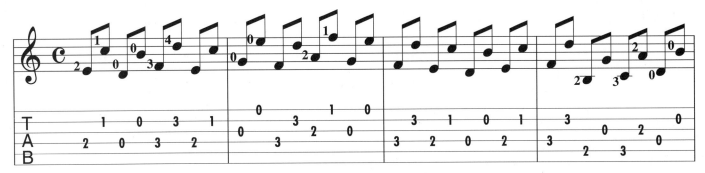

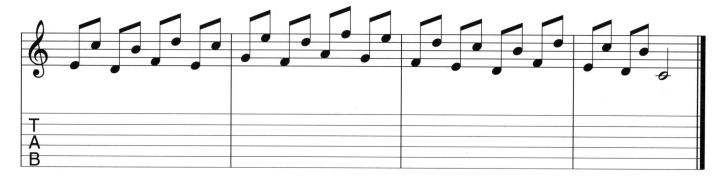

THE TENTH

The tenth, also known as a compound third, uses ten degrees of the diatonic scale or one octave i.e. C-C plus one third C-E.

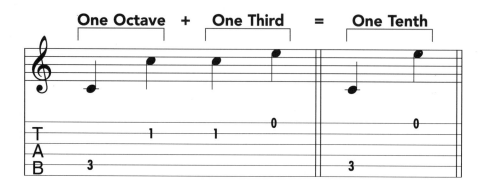

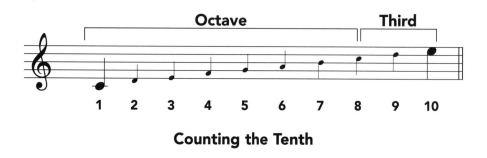

Counting the Tenth

71.0 Study (10ths)   Carcassi

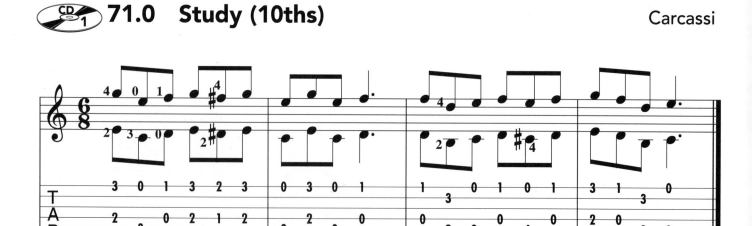

3RDS, 6THS, 10THS AND OCTAVES

The following piece clearly demonstrates the combined use of these intervals.

72. Study in C Major

Carcassi

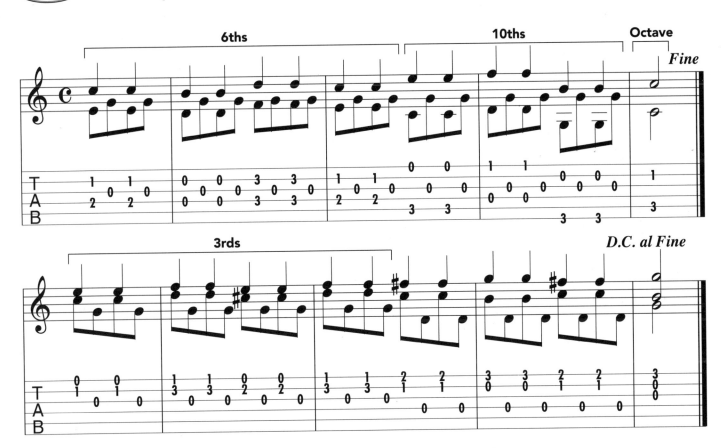

REST STROKE AND FREE STROKE IN COMBINATION

The above piece can serve to introduce the student to the important technique of using a rest stroke, most commonly on the highest or melody note, to accentuate the melody and help to separate it from the free stroke accompaniment. Practice this piece (and subsequent pieces) using first free stroke and then rest stroke on the melody notes, without changing right hand position. In the above piece, rest strokes can be applied to all notes with the stems pointing upwards on line one.

Try applying this technique to pieces already studied in the book, i.e. **Waltz** page 66 , **Sakura** page 79.

IMPORTANT NOTE

The following section on **Unison Notes** takes the student out of the first position in order to explain the concept of notes of the same pitch, i.e. highness or lowness of a note, on different strings and positions. By now the student should be competent enough to understand and execute the examples whilst using this section as a reference for learning the fingerboard in conjunction with the study of **positions** to follow.

LEARNING THE FINGERBOARD

UNISON NOTES

Because each fret on the fingerboard marks the distance of a semitone, wherever a string is stopped at any fret, the next fret stopped either above or below is a semitone, as it is from an open string to the first fret. Therefore due to the nature of the guitar's tuning, by stopping the sixth string at the fifth fret, we obtain the A which is a **unison** of the open fifth string A. Similarly, if we stop the sixth string at the sixth fret, we obtain the A♯ (B♭) which is a unison of the fifth string, first fret A♯ (B♭). This system is the same for all strings except the third string, which must be stopped four frets above the second string. The following examples show the system of unison notes as they shift up the fingerboard on to the next lower string (as demonstrated on the accompanying **Table of Unisons** page 95).

Note: refer to **Appendix One**, page 203, "Tuning the Guitar to Itself".

UNISON EXAMPLES

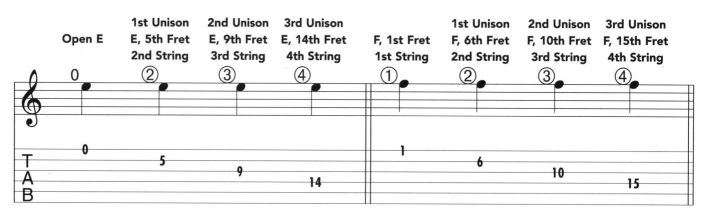

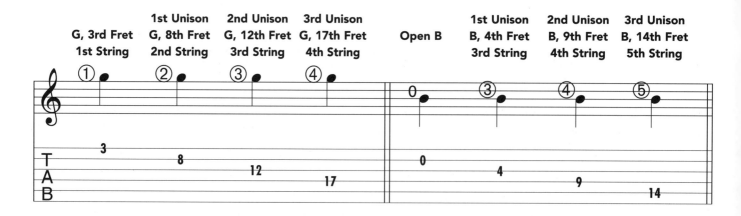

The following pieces which have already been studied earlier in the **first position** (page 22 and 24) are now demonstrated in the **fifth position** (**first unison**) and the **ninth position** (**second unison**). Remember that **position** indicates the **fret controlled by the first finger**.

CD 1 73.0 Ode to Joy (First Unison)

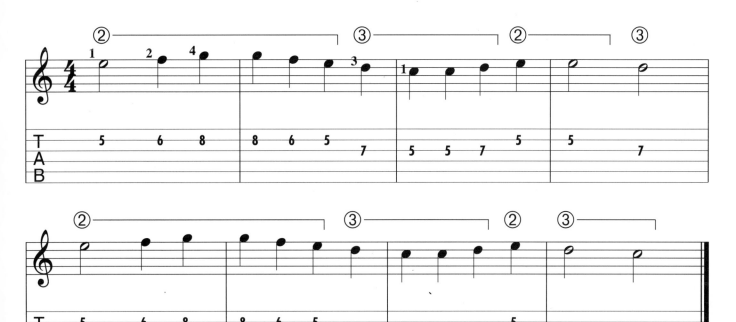

CD 1 73.1 Ode to Joy (Second Unison)

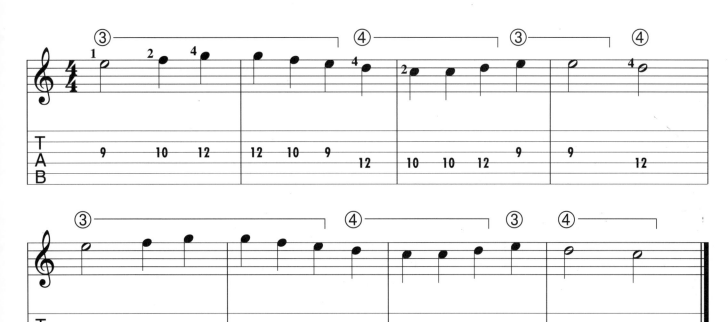

74.0 Jingle Bells (First Unison)

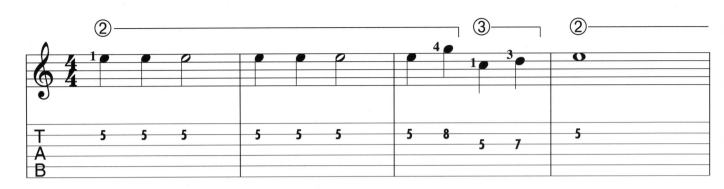

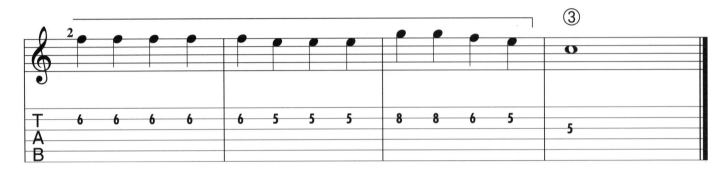

 74.1 Jingle Bells (Second Unison)

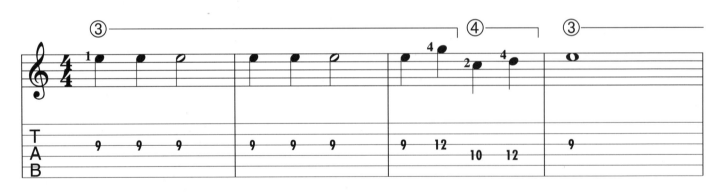

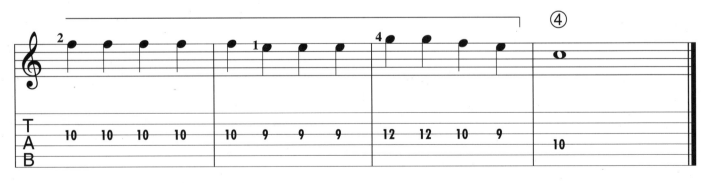

The following table shows the notes on the guitar fingerboard and how the unison system works via the six open strings and the notes above E on the first string. This table can be used as a reference for finding the notes on the fingerboard easily.

Note: dotted indication relates to unison examples (page 92) and pieces (page 93 and 94).

TABLE OF UNISONS

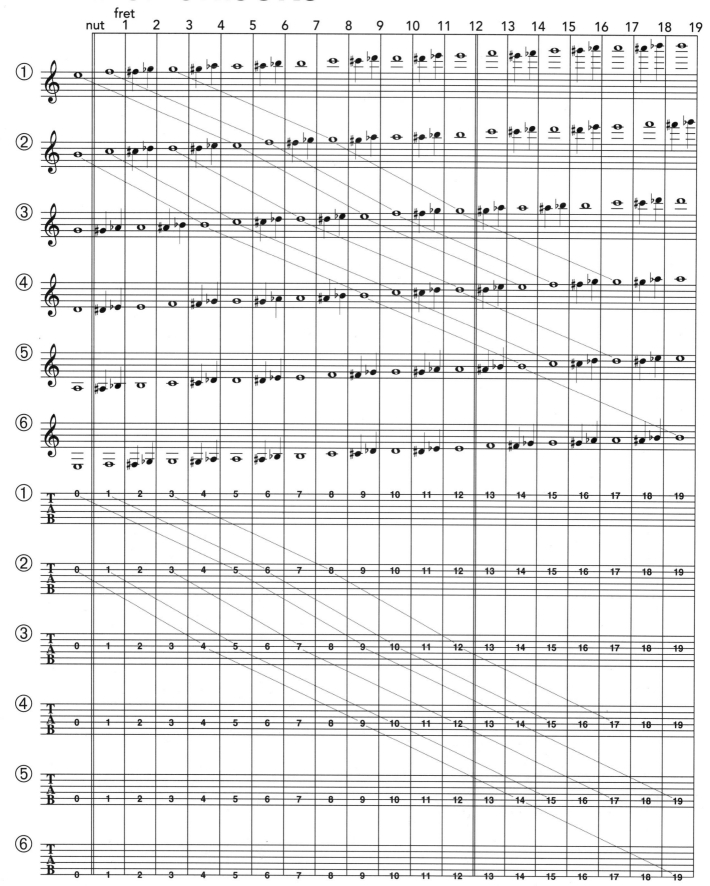

NEW POSITIONS

THE SECOND POSITION

Until now, only the notes on frets 1, 2, 3 and 4 have been used and this constitutes the **first position**, i.e. meaning that the first finger plays the notes on the first fret (F on ①, C on ②, G♯ on ③ etc.). Position can therefore be considered taken from whichever fret the first finger is controlling. When the first finger shifts upwards one fret (F♯ on ①, C♯ on ②, A on ③ etc.), this then constitutes the **second position**. This shift enables the fourth finger to comfortably reach the new notes on the fifth fret as shown below.

Position is normally indicated by **Roman numerals**, i.e. **second position = II**.
The Bar or half Bar substitutes for a position as it automatically indicates the use of the first finger on that particular fret.

Apart from the new note A on fifth fret ①, all of these notes have been studied in the first position, but as has been explained in the section on unisons, the same note (in pitch) can be found on the next lower string by moving up the fretboard, 5 frets on ⑥ ⑤ ④ and ②, 4 frets on ③.

FIFTH FRET NOTES

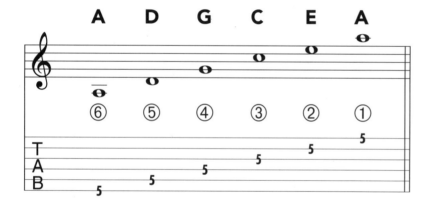

FIRST POSITION

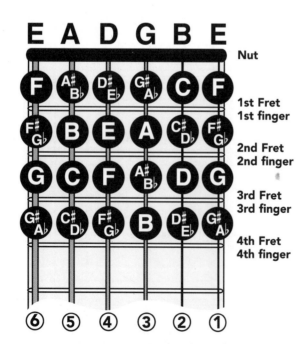

SECOND POSITION

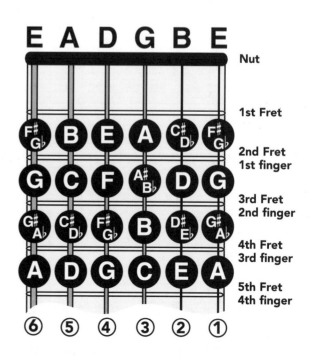

THE SHIFT FROM 1ST TO 2ND POSITION

In the following **two octave A melodic minor scale**, the first finger must shift to the **second position** (F#) in order to comfortably accommodate the upper notes when ascending, and return to **first position** (F♮) when descending. A new note is introduced by nature of this shift, this being A, fifth fret, first string (①). Remember to move the thumb with the first finger as described on page 18.

TWO OCTAVE A MELODIC MINOR SCALE

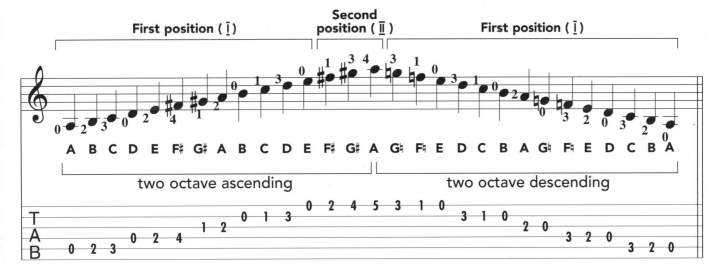

THE GUIDE FINGER

Make sure to leave the first finger on the ① F#, and the third finger on the ① G# until the ① A is used when fingering the ascending scale. Once the A has been played and lifted, without leaving the string slide the first and third fingers lightly down one fret to the first position, and complete the scale on ① G♮ and F♮. This method of moving a finger or fingers by lightly sliding up or down the string from one fret to another is called a **guide finger**. **Guide fingers** are sometimes indicated by a line (—) between the two notes.

The following keys of **D major** and **B minor** are primarily in the **second position**, and are therefore excellent for demonstrating its use.

KEY OF D MAJOR

FIRST POSITION D MAJOR SCALE
(two sharps, F# and C# in key signature)

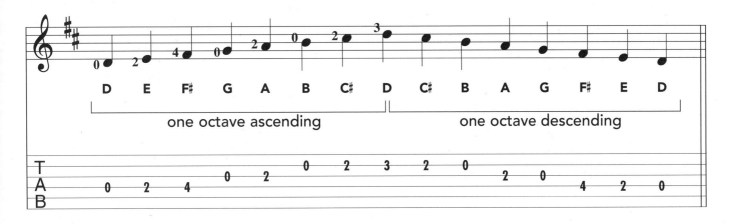

SECOND POSITION D MAJOR SCALE

Using alternative fingering (without open strings) and introducing new fifth fret notes **D** on ⑤, **G** on ④.

EXTENDED SECOND POSITION D MAJOR SCALE

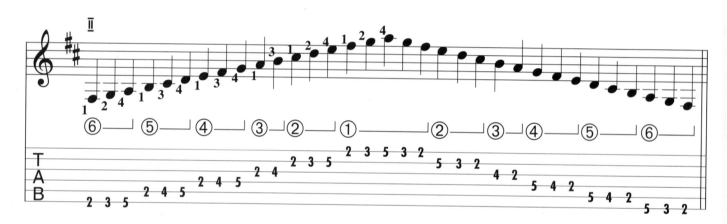

 **75.**

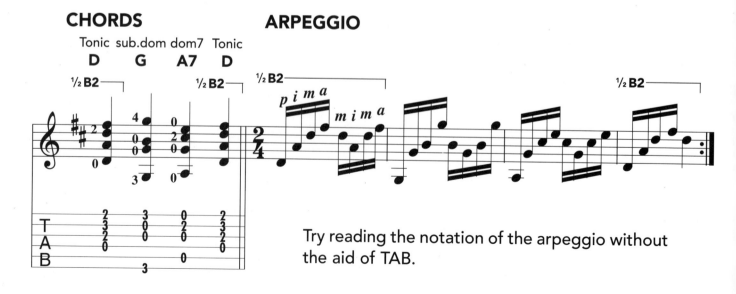

Try reading the notation of the arpeggio without the aid of TAB.

DEMONSTRATING THE SECOND POSITION

The famous melody of **Ode to Joy** is used to demonstrate the notes in the **second position**. Note also that the TAB has been omitted on the second line of each example as the notation should be easily recognizable at this stage.

76.0   Ode to Joy (using ① and ②)

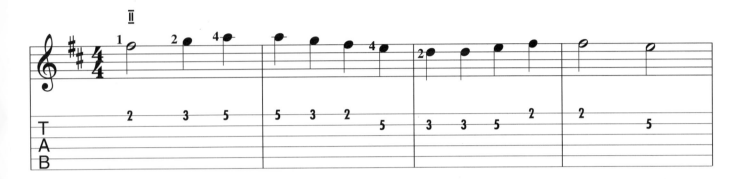

76.1   Ode to Joy (using ③, ④ and ⑤)

77. Prelude in D

Carulli

At bar 15, the right hand picking pattern changes from *pimipi* to *pimimi*. In bars 13-18 the **second finger** is used as a **guide** and a **pivot**, remaining on the second string.

 **78. Rondo** (a form of music, based on the principle of a return to an initial theme) Carcassi

Note: TAB is not used on repeated lines.

LISTENING TO MUSIC

It is important for the student to listen to quality music at every opportunity, guitar or non-guitar, in order to build up his or her knowledge and appreciation of music. As for the guitar, I would recommend recordings (the great majority of which are only available on vinyl) of the great players Segovia, Diaz, Bream and Williams made between the 1950's and the 1980's, as this constitutes, in my opinion, the great period of playing and recording the mainstream repertoire.

KEY OF B MINOR

B MELODIC MINOR SCALE
(relative to D, two sharps, F♯ and C♯ in key signature)

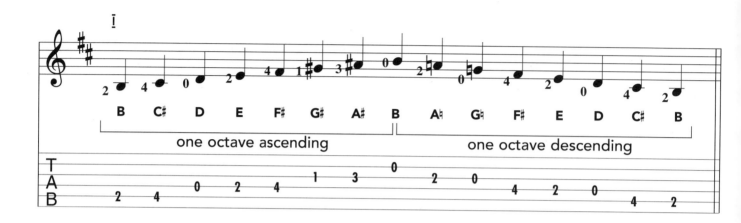

In the following chords and arpeggio exercise leave the **B2** in position for both the F♯7 and Bm chords.

 **79.**

CHORDS   **ARPEGGIO**

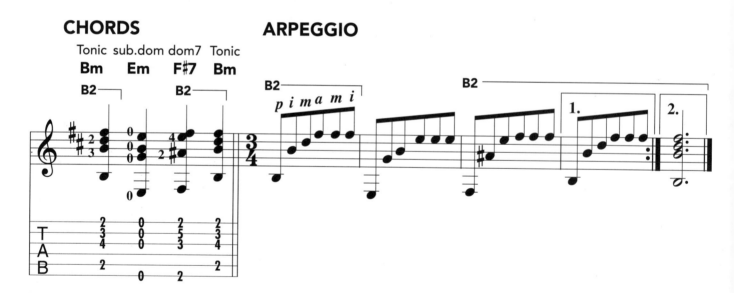

The key of B minor was a particular favourite of the great Andres Segovia, and he composed several important studies in this key. Agustin Barrios also chose B minor as the key for his greatest work, **La Catedral**.

In Sor's **Study in B Minor**, (on the following page) I have only included the first section to demonstrate the key of B minor and Bar chords. Try using **rest strokes** (see page 91) on the upper or melody notes, i.e. first and third beats of each bar, to give a texture to the otherwise sameness of the arpeggio. Make sure to retain the correct hand position when using the rest stroke. As it is an arpeggio study you should hold chord shapes wherever possible. In bars 1 - 6 the **third finger** acts as a **pivot** (dotted indication).

80. Study in B Minor (Duet)

Sor

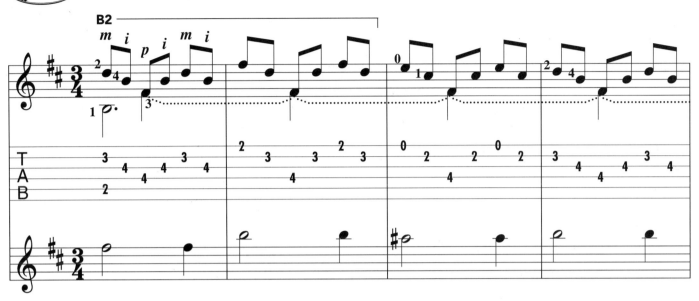

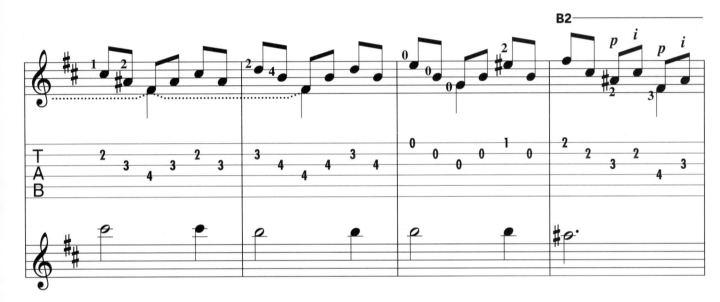

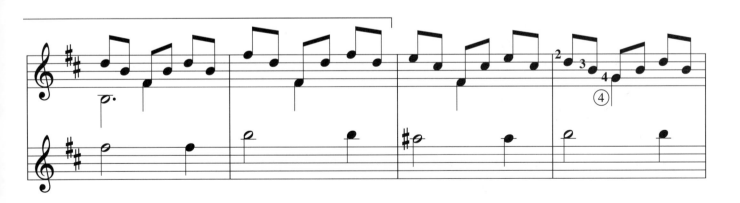

TONE, TEMPO AND DYNAMICS

TONE

A **Tone** has four characteristics: **pitch, duration, dynamics** and **timbre**.

Pitch: The highness or lowness of a **tone**.
Duration: The length of a **tone**.
Dynamics: The force or power of a **tone** (loudness or softness).
Timbre: Quality of the **tone**.

A **note** represents the **pitch** and **duration** of a **tone**.

THE TEMPO (speed)

The tempo indicates the pace of the piece or movement, usually written above the staff at the beginning:

Largo, Adagio = very slow
Andante = slow
Andantino = medium slow
Moderato = at a moderate rate of speed
Allegretto = medium fast

Allegro = fast
Vivace = lively, quick
Presto = very fast
Meno mosso = slower
Piu mosso = faster

Modifications of speed inside of one or more measures are indicated by:

- *Ritardando (rit.)* or *Rallentando (rall.)* = gradually slower
- *Accelerando (accel.)* = gradually faster (accelerate) is usually followed by a change in tempo
- *A tempo* = to play at the previous speed
- *The Fermata* or *Pause* ⌒ above or below a note means that it is to be sustained longer than its indicated value

Some other commonly used musical terms or marks:

- *Da Capo (D.C.)* = from the beginning
- *Da Capo al Fine (D.C. al Fine)* = from the beginning to *Fine* (end)
- *Dal Segno* 𝄋 = repeat from the sign, usually as far as the *Fine* or as far as the *Coda Sign* ⊕ , then skip to the appended ending of the piece marked *Coda* (lit. tail).

DYNAMICS (different degrees of loudness and softness)

Letters and signs used to indicate different degrees of loudness:

- *p* = piano, soft
- *pp* = piannisimo, very soft
- *f* = forte, loud
- *ff* = fortissimo, very loud
- *mf* = mezzoforte, moderately loud
- *poco a poco* = little by little
- *cresc.* or < = crescendo, increasing the sound gradually
- *dim., decresc.* or > = diminuendo, decrescendo, diminishing the sound gradually
- *sf, sfz* = sforzando, sforzato, give sudden emphasis to the note or chord
- *fp* = forte-piano, loud and immediately soft again

The following pieces, although both marked **Andante** (or relatively slow) should be played quite differently in style and feel.

Carulli's **Andante** is in the style of the **Siciliene** which is an old dance of Sicilian origin in a lilting $\frac{6}{8}$ time. Sor's **Andante**, however, is in an almost march like $\frac{4}{4}$ time and should be played quite rigidly. Both pieces are primarily in the **first position** with occasional shifts to the **second position** (marked $\overline{\text{II}}$).

Note: the use of **dynamics** and **tempo markings** throughout both pieces and selected pieces to follow.

81. **Andante** - **1st and 2nd positions**   Carulli

(Guide fingers, see page 97)

DOUBLE DOTTING

As has been demonstrated previously, a dot after a note increases the value of the note by half (see page 12). A second dot (placed after the first) increases the value of the note by half the value of the first dot.

i.e. ♩. = ♩♪ : a dotted crotchet equals a crotchet plus a quaver.

♩.. = ♩♪♬ : a double dotted crotchet equals a crotchet plus a quaver plus a semi quaver.

This formula is the same for all note values.

CD 1 82. Andante - 1st and 2nd positions   Sor

LIGADO TECHNIQUE

Ligado is used primarily to acquire a smooth continuity when playing groups of notes and also allows faster playing when required. This technique is also called **hammer**, **snap** or **slur**.

ASCENDING LIGADO (upwards slur or hammer)

The **ascending ligado** (indicated by ⌒) is achieved by hammering any left hand finger on to the required note either from an open string, i.e. **Exercise A**, or from a lower finger, i.e. **Exercise B**. It is also necessary to prepare the **ligado finger** somewhat further from the fretboard than normal in order to achieve the required strength for the hammer.

Note: • move only the finger, keep the hand completely steady.

• remember to alternate R/H fingers on each plucked or "pre-ligado" note.

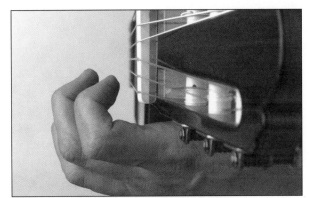

first finger preparation

completion

83. **Exercise A**

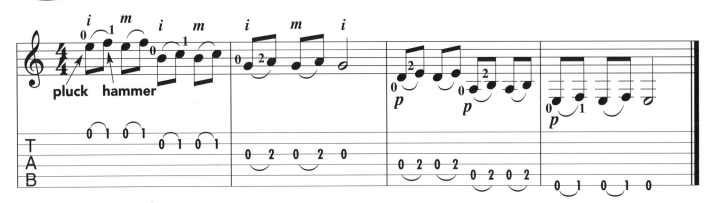

84. **Exercise B**

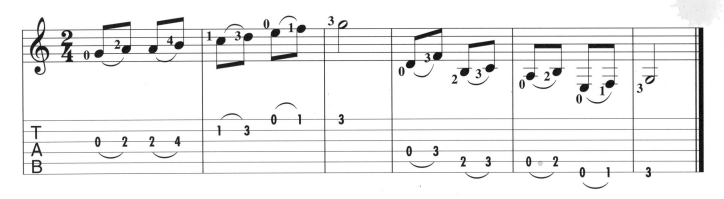

DESCENDING LIGADO *(downwards slur or snap)*

The **descending ligado** (indicated by ⌢) is achieved by snapping any left hand finger onto an open string, i.e. **Exercise A**, or from a higher finger on to a lower finger, **Exercise B**. Make sure to anchor the lower or holding finger and pull the ligado finger sideways without distorting the note.

Observe the following:

1. Prepare both left hand fingers on the string together, except of course when onto an open string.

2. The lower or holding finger must press firmly and should not be pulled aside by the action of the ligado finger.

3. When used on an inside string, i.e. ② - ⑥, the ligado finger executes the snap and comes to rest against the adjacent string, i.e. after the ligado is used on ② the finger rests briefly against ①. This same technique is employed when more than two notes are joined by the ligado sign.

Note: move only the finger, keep the hand completely steady.

first finger preparation

completion

85. Exercise A

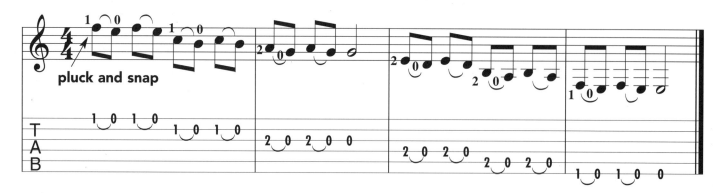

86. Exercise B

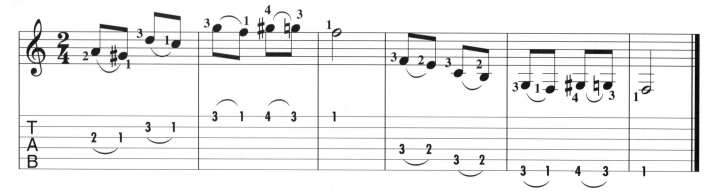

LIGADO STUDIES

Practice the following studies on all strings remembering to adjust the left hand as it moves from ① - ⑥ as explained on page 31.

 **87.0**

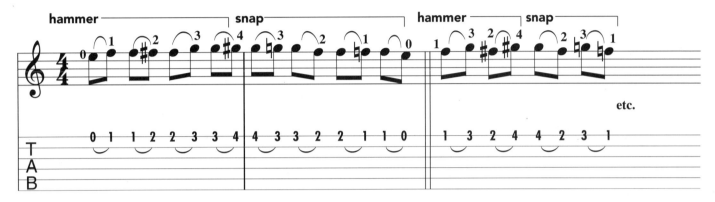

 **87.1 Duet in C** - using first position ligados — Kuffner

Some of the notation of this piece contains Tab and some does not. It alternates line by line, i.e: the first line contains Tab but the second line doesn't. The third line contains Tab but the fourth line doesn't.

Duet in C continues over page...

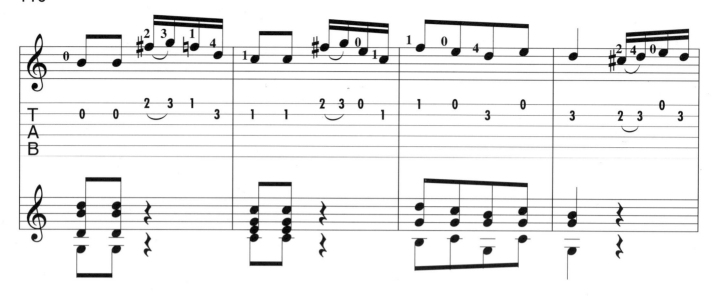

D.C. al Fine

88. Ligado Study in 1st and 2nd position

Carulli

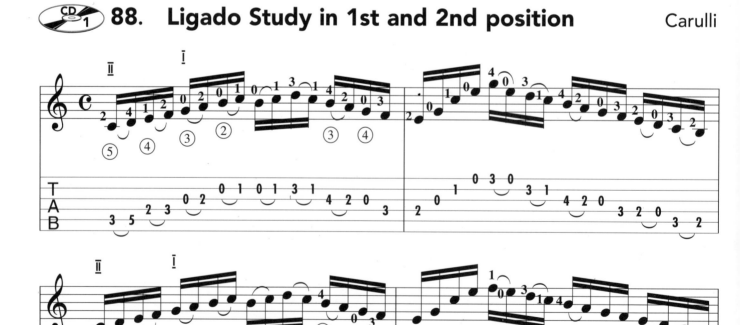

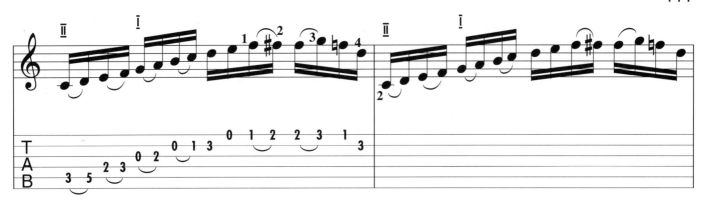

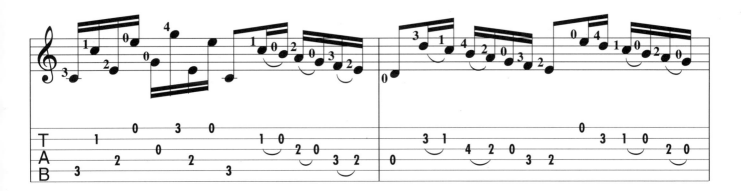

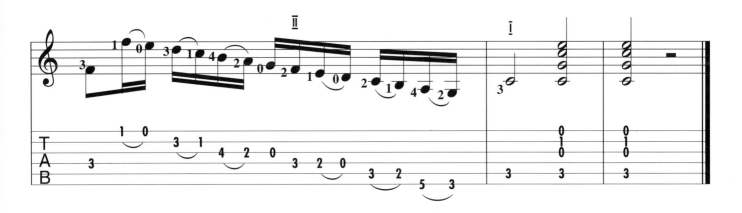

The following study is primarily in the **second position** with only occasional notes in the **first position**. Be sure to alternate the right hand fingers and keep the left hand steady when using ligados i.e. move only the fingers as explained on page 107.

89. Study in Ligados

Carulli

112

D.C. al Fine

The following **Right Hand Studies** should be practiced at various tempi. Use first free and then rest strokes on the melody (*a* finger) notes.

 90. **Right Hand Studies**

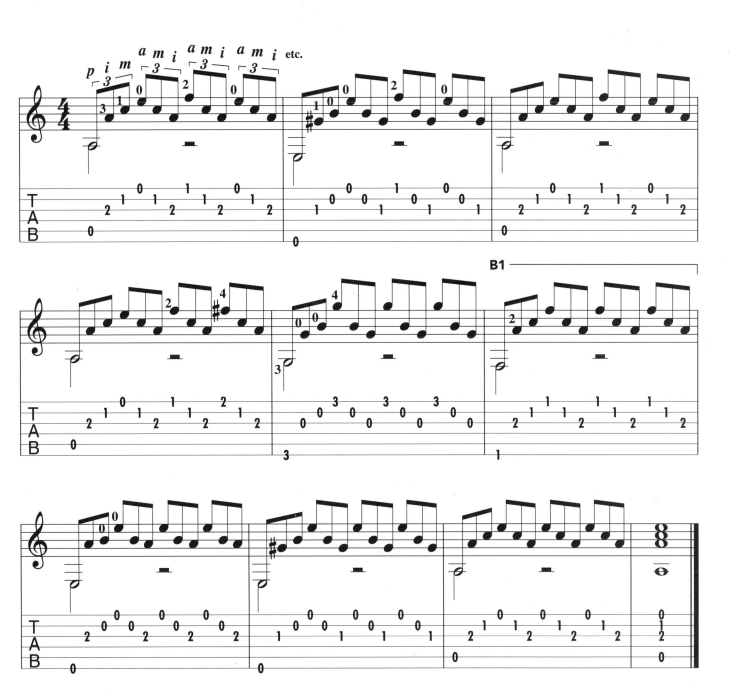

Var. 1   **Var. 2**   **Var. 3**

THE ROUND ARPEGGIO

Another important variation that can be included using the previous example is the **round arpeggio**. This arpeggio has been used by several important composers from Sor, Aguado, Giuliani, Carulli etc. in the classic period through to Villa-Lobos in the twentieth century.

In order to achieve an effective **round arpeggio**, grip the right hand fingers on their respective strings, i.e. *i* on ③, *m* on ② and *a* on ① and, after having plucked with *p*, release *i* whilst still gripping *m* and *a*. Follow by releasing *m* and finally *a*. On the return part of the arpeggio, *m* and *i* pluck without gripping as shown in the example below. Obviously, this should be practiced slowly before working up to the desired speed.

Note: the round arpeggio is notated as 6 sixteenth notes (⌐⁶¬).

 **91.0**

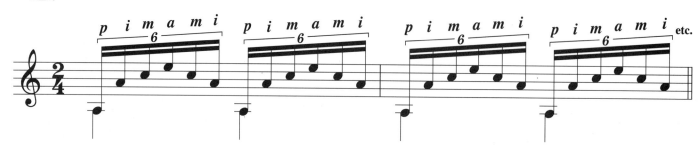

 **91.1** **Prelude in A Minor** (using Round Arpeggio)   Carulli

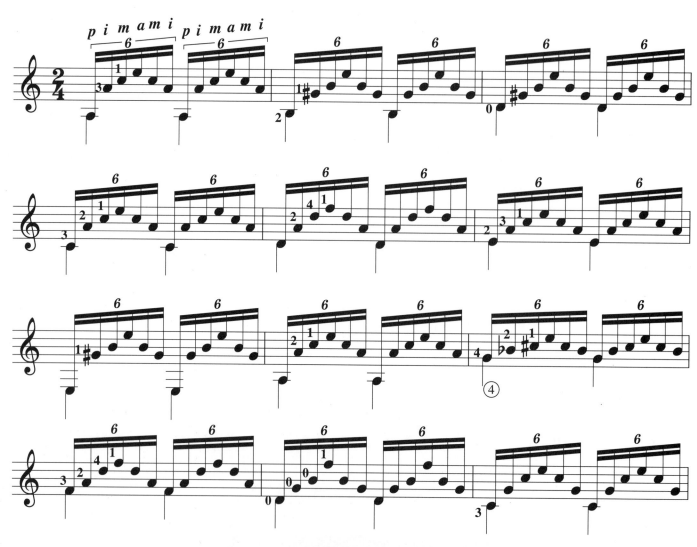

BROKEN CHORDS

The very beautiful and extensively used effect of **broken chords** is based on the technique used in the ***p i m a*** section of the above round arpeggio. This **harp-like** effect is often used in place of a block chord (i.e. with all notes played together) and is seldom indicated but left up to the players discretion. As described above, ***p i m*** and ***a*** grip the required strings and are released at the desired speed, which can vary immensely. The required effect is for the highest (or last) note to sound on the beat, which means the preceding notes are to be played slightly before the beat.

BLOCK CHORD

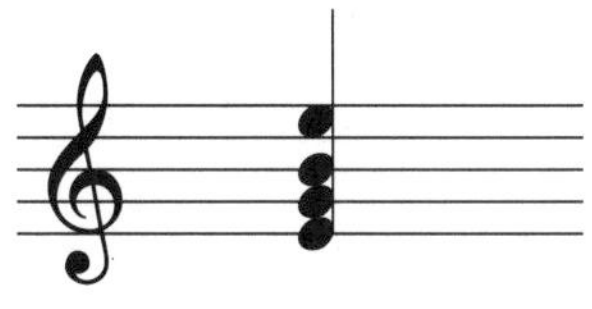

BROKEN CHORD
The notation could be indicated as:
Listen carefully to the recording
for the desired effect.

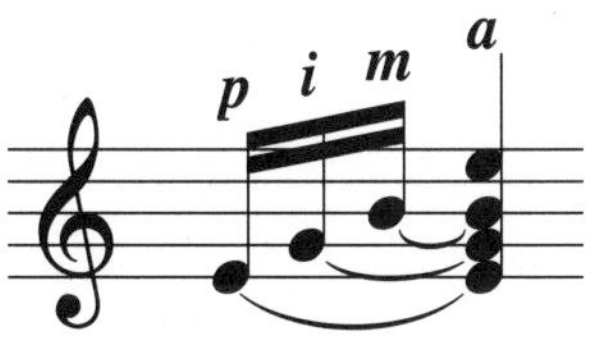

CD 1 **92.**

BLOCK CHORDS **BROKEN CHORDS**

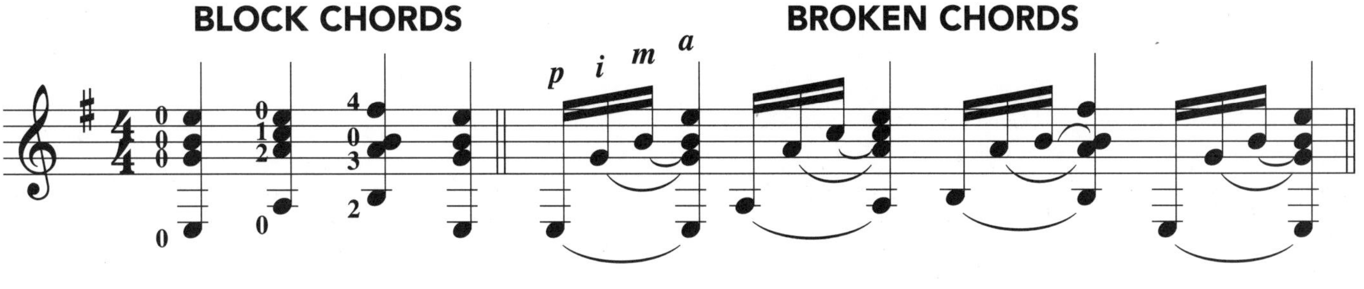

The following study is excellent for developing the **full Bar** in conjunction with the frequently used **A** and **D** chord shapes. Be sure to retain a straight Bar finger and do not lose the bass note as the chord changes are made. It is important to push the second finger close to the fret on each change and do not allow it to fall towards the third finger.

ASCENDING FULL BAR STUDY

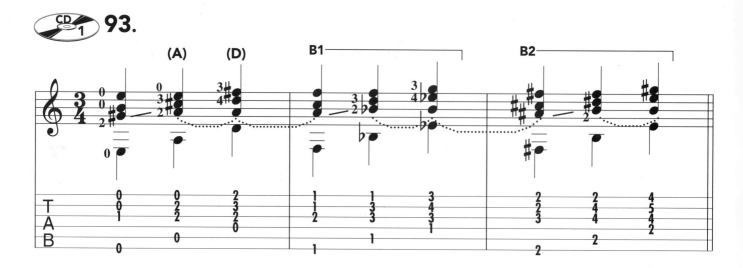

Once the above study has been memorized various right hand arpeggio patterns can be substituted as shown below and it can be continued up the fretboard.

KEY OF A MAJOR
TWO OCTAVE A MAJOR SCALE
(3 sharps, F#, C# and G# in key signature)

CD 1 94.0

CHORDS

Tonic sub.dom dom7 Tonic
A   D   E7   A

ARPEGGIO

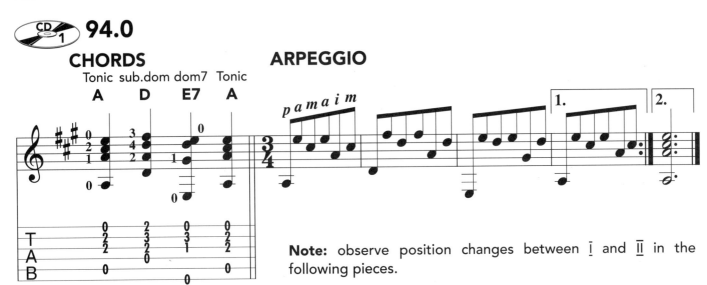

Note: observe position changes between Ⅰ and Ⅱ in the following pieces.

CD 1 94.1 Study in A

Giuliani

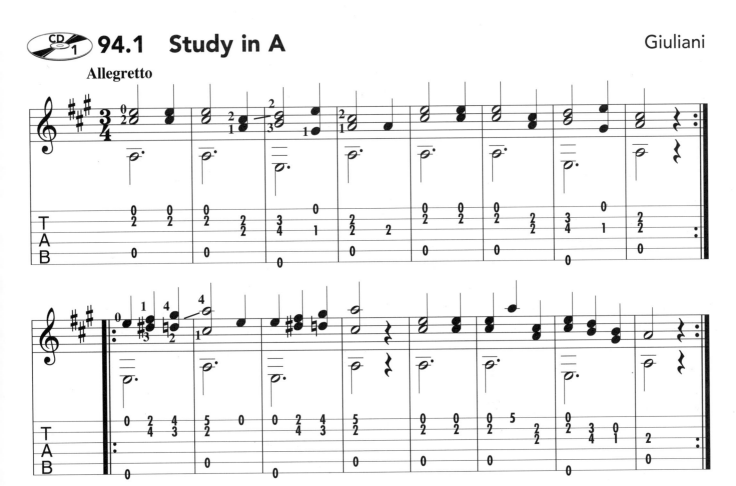

95. Study in A

Carulli

ORNAMENTS

Ornaments are also called **embellishments** or **graces** (meaning to decorate the melody). The subject of ornamentation is a large one because of the vast number of forms, periods of music etc., and only the more common types will be explained in this method.

Dance in A, (pg 119) introduces the **acciaccatura** or **crushed note** which is commonly used in guitar music as a **grace note**. Almost no time is taken for its performance with virtually no shortening of the main (or principal) note and the beat must fall on the main note. The acciaccatura is a form of ligado, and therefore the previously practiced technique of the snap must be observed (see page 108). Further ornaments will be explained as they are encountered in the method.

*Note: the use of the thirty-second note ♪ which is worth an eighth of a beat. Eight thirty-second notes equal one quarter note.

e.g.

96. Dance in A

Giuliani

KEY OF F♯ MINOR
F♯ MELODIC MINOR SCALE
(relative to A, three sharps, F♯, C♯ and G♯ in key signature)

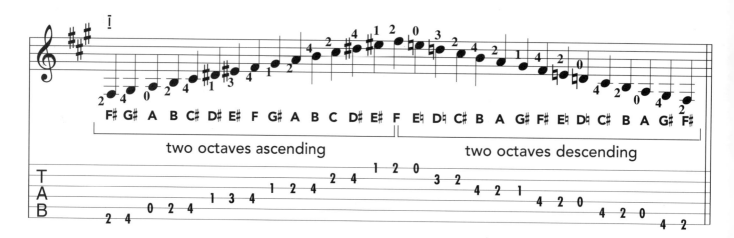

CD 1 **97.0**

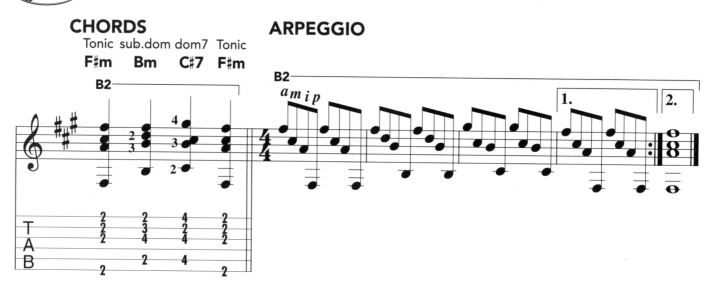

The following **study** uses an interesting **dotted eighth note** rhythm (see page 70) primarily on the second string whilst upper and lower voices are presented as dotted minims. Try practising the voicing separately before playing the piece together.

CD 1 **97.1 Study in F♯m**

Nemerowski

Note: the dotted minims are to be played together with the dotted quavers at the beginning of each bar.

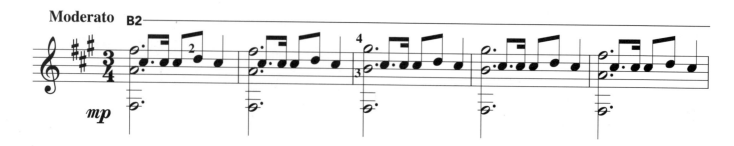

SECTION 3

THE FIFTH POSITION

Now that you have thoroughly explored the notes in the **first** and **second positions**, it is time to move to the important and frequently used **fifth position** (indicated as $\underline{V}$). The notes on the fifth fret have been used in the second position by the fourth finger, but by shifting to the fifth position it is now possible to play as far as the eighth fret as seen below.

Examples, scales and pieces commonly used in the fifth position, i.e. using first unison notes, will be demonstrated.

NEW NOTES ON FRETS 6, 7 AND 8

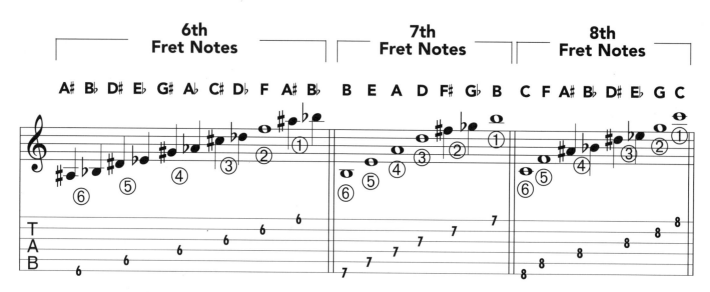

FIFTH POSITION

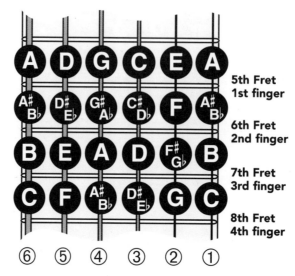

FIFTH POSITION SCALES (One octave)

C Major Scale on ③ ② and ①   C Major Scale on ⑥ ⑤ and ④

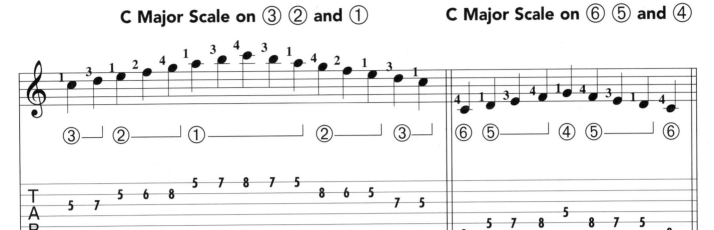

EXTENDED FIFTH POSITION F MAJOR SCALE

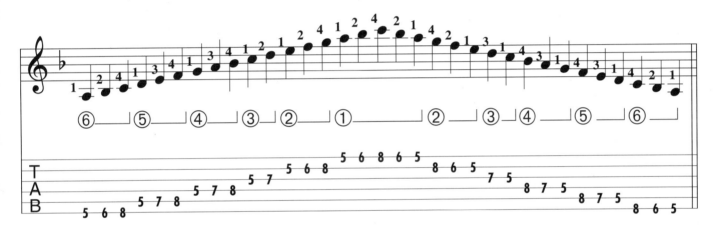

POSITION SHIFTS USING FIRST UNISON NOTES

The following **two octave C major scale** uses the two new notes on the first string; **B** (7th fret) and **C** (8th fret) by means of a shift to the **fifth position** (i.e. first finger to fifth fret ③). This is therefore a shift to the **first unison C**, the fifth position also providing first unison notes D (on ③) and E, F and G (on ②). The shift from open B ② to fifth position C ③ (first unison) is a common and convenient way to move up and down the fingerboard and will often be used for the duration of this method.

TWO OCTAVE C MAJOR SCALE

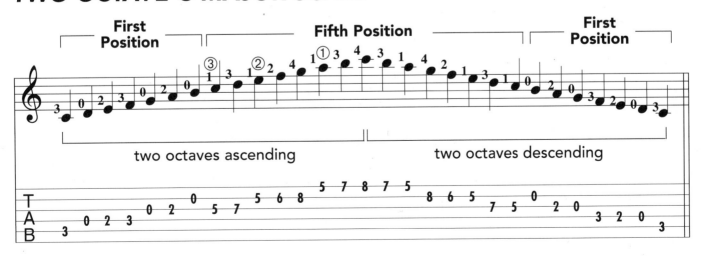

DEMONSTRATING THE FIFTH POSITION

 **98. Jingle Bells**

 99. Ode to Joy (duet)

Beethoven

1. Asturias (fifth position)

Albeniz

TRANSCRIPTION

Asturias, originally composed for the piano by the Spaniard, Isaac Albeniz (1860 - 1909), is a typical example of a **transcription**, meaning to arrange the piece for a different instrument. The guitar relies heavily on transcriptions by nature of its small repertoire, and it is advisable for the student to study the original version, both music manuscript and recordings, wherever possible.

126

The following piece is entirely in the **fifth position** apart from the fourth to last bar where it temporarily uses the **first position** (marked Ī) before returning to V̄.

Remember to remain in the fifth position as the open B notes are played and use *p* to play bass notes on ④.

2. Minuet in A Minor (Duet)

J.S.Bach

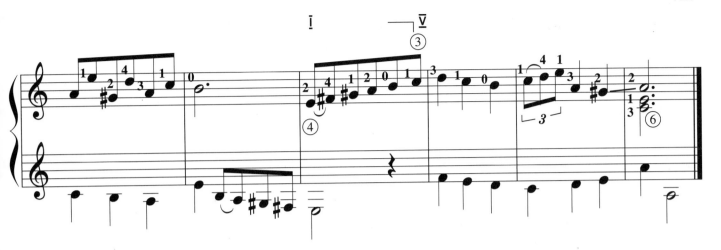

The following studies by the great Spanish guitarist, Francisco Tarrega, are excellent for demonstrating smooth shifts between the **first**, **second** and **fifth positions**. Both studies use Bars and half-Bars and a number of guide fingers as indicated i.e. 2 – 2 etc.. Practice using **rest strokes** on the notes marked ∇ throughout the pieces.

3. Study in C

Tarrega

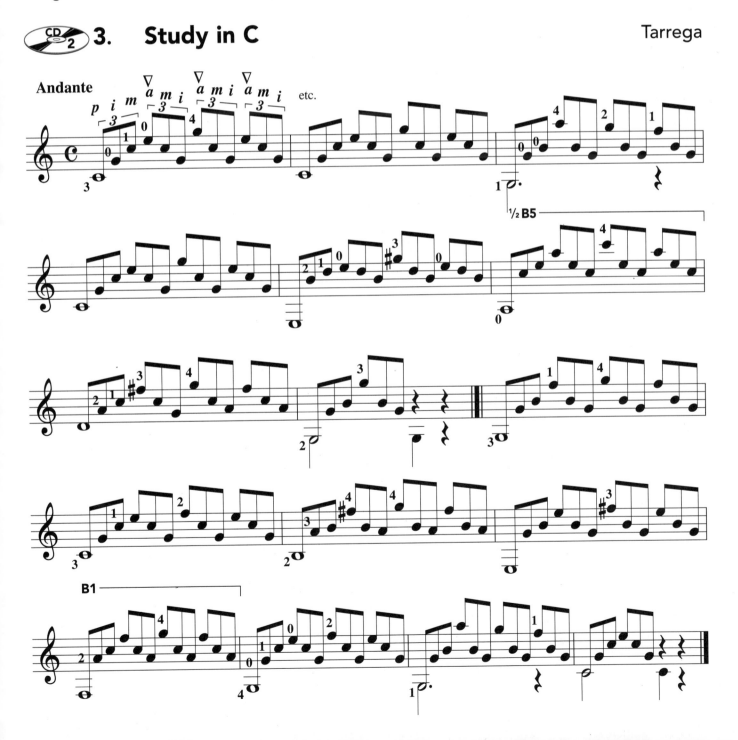

4. Study in Em

Tarrega

Var. 1   **Var. 2**   **Var. 3**   **Var. 4**

Niccolo Paganini, the renown 19th century violinist, also played the guitar and wrote extensively for the instrument.

This short **Andantino** demonstrates many of the techniques so far learned such as guides, round arpeggios, grace notes and position shifts.

5. Andantino

Paganini

CHROMATIC SCALE IN OCTAVES

The following **chromatic scale in octaves** is invaluable in establishing a steady left hand position. Move only the fingers and do not allow the left hand to shift out of the first position during the required stretches.

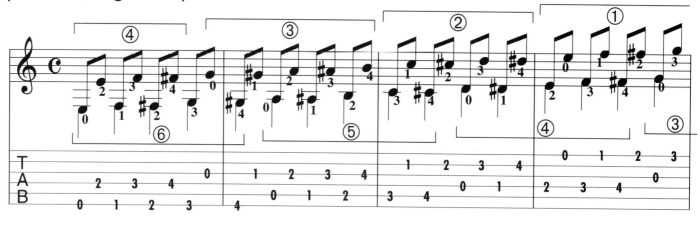

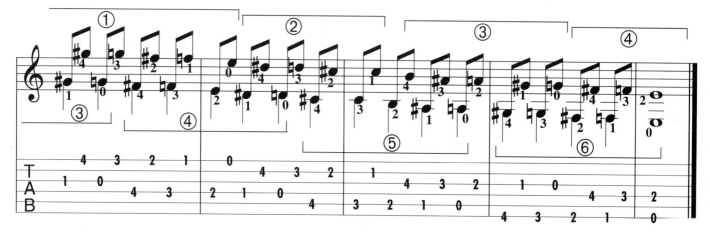

DIATONIC SCALE IN OCTAVES (to Fifth Position)

6. One Fine Day (Duet)

Puccini

KEY OF B♭ MAJOR
TWO OCTAVE B♭ MAJOR SCALE
(two flats, B♭ and E♭ in key signature)

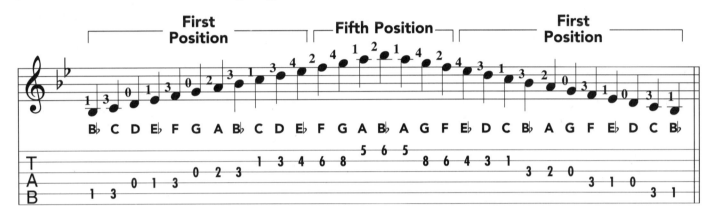

FIFTH POSITION TWO OCTAVE B♭ MAJOR SCALE

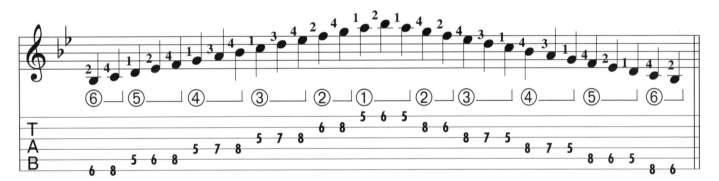

 **7.**

CHORDS   **ARPEGGIO**

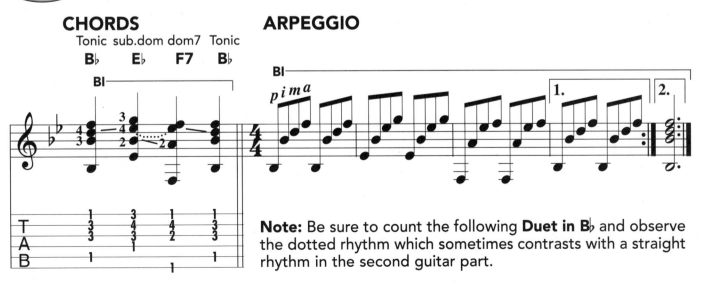

Note: Be sure to count the following **Duet in B♭** and observe the dotted rhythm which sometimes contrasts with a straight rhythm in the second guitar part.

8. Duet in B♭

Gaude

KEY OF G MINOR
TWO OCTAVE G MELODIC MINOR SCALE
(relative to B♭, two flats, B♭ and E♭ in key signature)

 9.

CHORDS

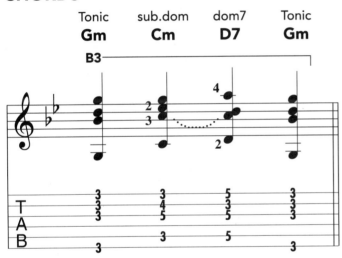

Note: introduction of **sixteenth note triplets** which are indicated as:

Sixteenth note triplets are played in the same time as two sixteenth notes.

ARPEGGIO

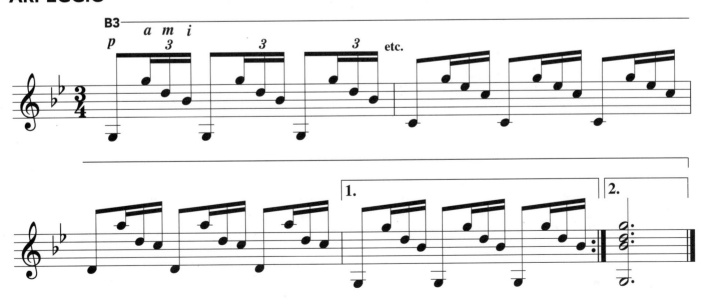

CD 2 **10. Study in Gm and B♭**   Ferandiere

The following study uses many familiar techniques, i.e. Bars and half Bars, ligados, guide fingers etc. It also features the **third position** (see **Gm** chords on previous page) and **sixteenth note triplets**.

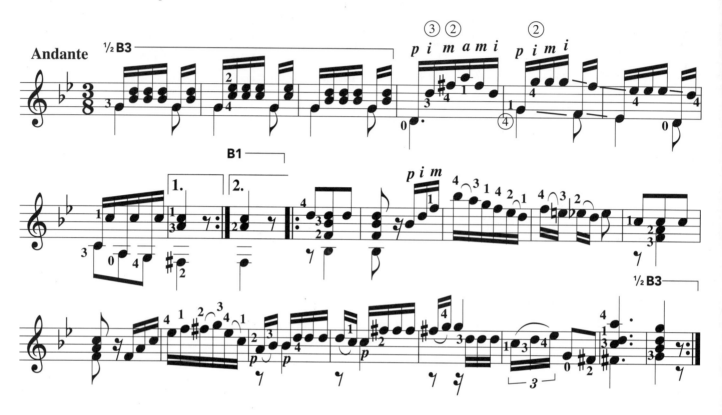

CD 2 **11. Study in G Minor**   Coste

THE SEVENTH POSITION
NEW NOTES ON FRETS 9 AND 10

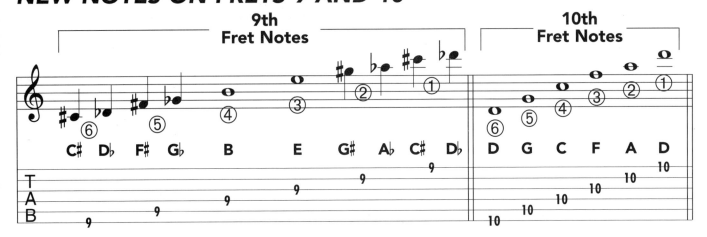

SEVENTH POSITION

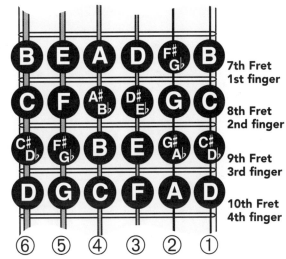

SEVENTH POSITION SCALES

D Major Scale on ③ ② and ①　　**D Major Scale on ⑥ ⑤ and ④**

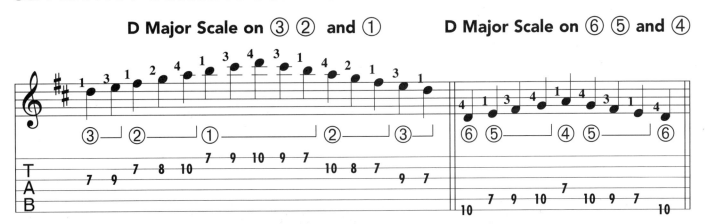

EXTENDED SEVENTH POSITION G MAJOR SCALE

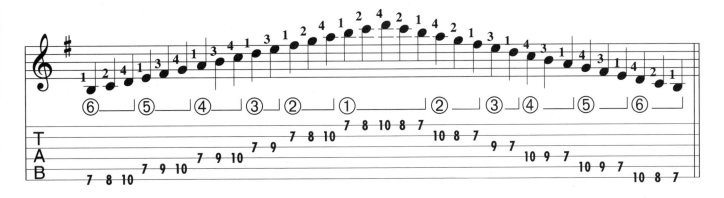

Try using the fingerings you have learnt in the higher positions to play the following:

CD 2 **12. Jesus Joy of Mans Desire** (Duet) J.S.Bach

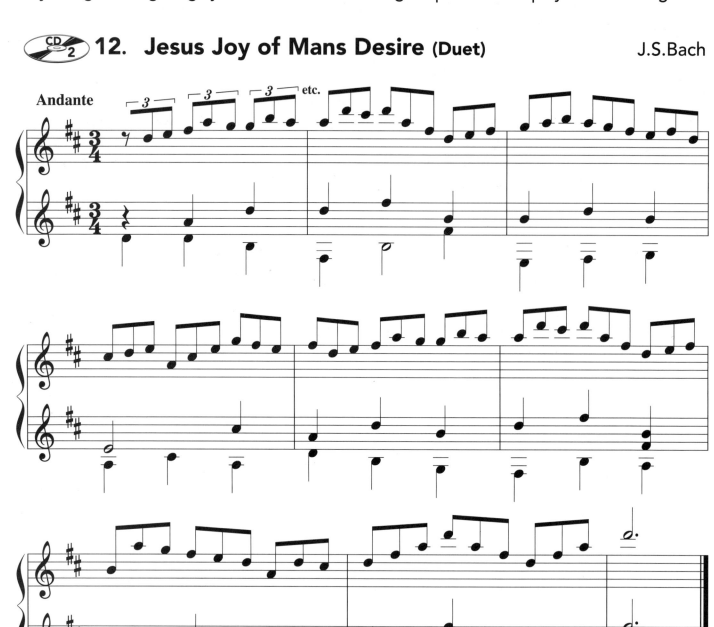

CD 2 **13. Asturias (seventh position)** Albeniz

Use the same fingering as that in fifth position **Asturias** (page 125).

The following demonstrates the concert version of **Asturias** using all of the required arpeggios which must be played according to the tempo dictated by the thumb. Listen carefully to the CD.

Note: sixteenth note triplets in variations 1, 2 and 3.

14. Asturias (Seventh Position)

Albeniz

SLIDE FINGER TECHNIQUES

Many beautiful sounds can be obtained by sliding the fingers along the strings to produce a vocal or typically stringed instrument effect. The **portamento** (or carrying the note) is a subtle effect rather like the guide finger (see page 97) whereby a finger (or fingers) move from one note to the next, lightly sounding the notes in between. The **slide** works the same, however, the finger (or fingers) press the string harder and therefore sound the notes in between. Whereas the portamento is seldom indicated but more often assumed, the slide is indicated by a line i.e. 2 – 2.

Listen carefully to the following **Moderato in C**, bars 1 and 5 for the difference between the two effects. **Moderato in C** also uses the **seventh position** ($\overline{VII}$), as well as the **full Bar 5** to demonstrate **first unison** notes on ② ③ ④ and ⑤.

15. Moderato in C   Sor

16. Minuet in C   Sor

*   Use *p* to brush across ⑥ - ①
**   Play as grace notes, i.e. E, B and G played together followed rapidly by F, G hammers, G to F snap.
***   Use of Fermata (⌢), meaning to hold the note to the players own discretion (also called pause sign, see page 104)

KEY OF E MAJOR

FIRST POSITION EXTENDED, TWO OCTAVE E MAJOR SCALE
(four sharps, F♯, C♯, G♯ and D♯ in key signature)

 **17.**

CHORDS

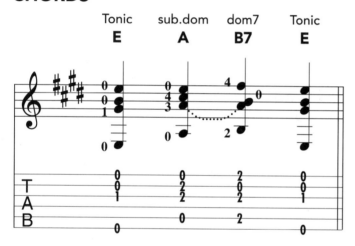

ARPEGGIO

Execute this arpeggio by gripping *i m a* on ③ ② and ① before playing each group as explained on page 115.

The following **E major Study** clearly demonstrates the common chord sequence, **E** (tonic Ī), **A** (sub. dom. ĪV), **B7** (dom. 7th V̄ 7), **E** (tonic Ī), as explained on page 140. Take special care to tie the F♯ using 3 on line 2, bar 3 for the required period of time. This passage is similar to that of the **B minor Study**, page 103, bar 1, where a tie is used on F♯ using 3.

18. 1st and 2nd Position, E major Study   Sor

FOURTH POSITION E MAJOR SCALE (practice also using **B4** throughout)

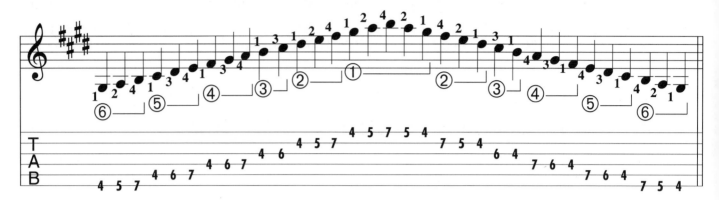

KEY OF C# MINOR
C# MELODIC MINOR SCALE
(relative to E, four sharps, F#, C#, G# and in D# in key signature)

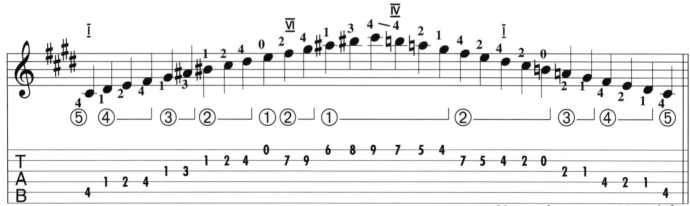

Note: observe position shifts

 **19.**

CHORDS

Fourth Position, E and B7 Chords
(ref. **study** page 143)

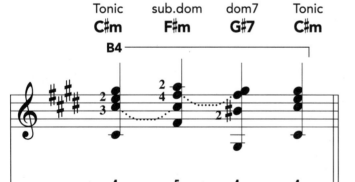

ARPEGGIO

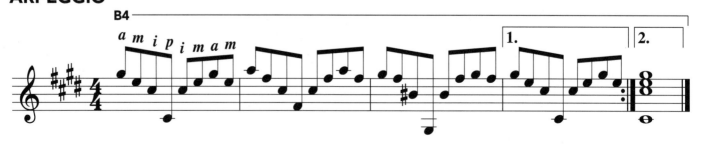

CD 2 20.0 4th Position, E and C♯m Study

Carulli

Use the **full Bar 4** for the entire study and finger according to the previous fourth position examples.

DEMONSTRATING THE USE OF THE BAR TO PLAY THE SAME PIECE IN A DIFFERENT KEY

Having thoroughly studied the previous piece using the **4th position Bar** throughout, it is now possible to play it in virtually every key by shifting the Bar up or down the fingerboard. Even the key of C can be used (Ex. 3) by thinking of the Bar finger as the nut of the guitar and using 2, 3 and 4 as the moving fingers. Only the keys of B♭ (A♯) and B present a problem, by virtue of the fact that it is not really feasible to Bar frets 11 and 12 because of the obstruction caused by the upper bout of the guitar body. The following exercises demonstrate the previous piece in the **second position** (key of D and Bm), **fifth position** (key of F and Dm) and the **open position** (key of C and Am) where the Bar finger is substituted by the nut.

Note: • 1 is not used in Ex.3.

• the process of changing from one key to another is called **transposition**.

PREVIOUS STUDY IN OTHER POSITIONS AND KEYS

💿₂ 20.1   2nd Position, D and Bm Study

Ex. 1

💿₂ 20.2   5th Position, F and Dm Study

Ex. 2

💿₂ 20.3   Open Position, C and Am Study (nut in place of Bar 1)

Ex. 3

CREATING VARIATIONS FROM AN EXISTING PIECE

It has been previously demonstrated (pg. 46 **Spanish Ballad**, pg. 113 **Right Hand Studies**, pg. 116 **Ascending Full Bar Study**, pg. 128 **Study in E minor**) that pieces with a consistent chord structure, once memorised, can be used to provide variations for the right hand, both in fingerings and rhythmic structure.

An excellent example is the following **Study in A minor** by Aguado, which was originally written as an arpeggio study as seen below in **Var. 1**. For the sake of this exercise, it has been written as block chords to be memorised before studying the variations.

Pieces such as this provide great value due to the fact that so much variation can immediately be applied to one memorised piece, rather than learning several similar pieces.

21. Study in A minor

Aguado

Note: For further study, refer to **Giuliani Right Hand Studies, Op.1**

DOUBLE SHARPS AND FLATS

The following duet introduces the **double sharp** (**X**) which raises the note a tone, i.e. the F double sharp in this case is the same as a G natural. The **double flat** (♭♭) works the same but by lowering the note a tone, i.e. A double flat equals G natural.

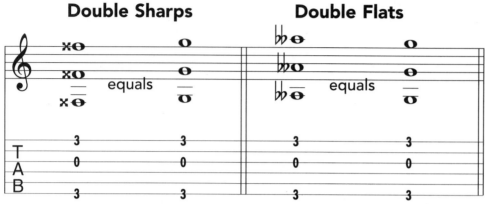

22. Duet in E

Carulli

SECTION 4

ALTERED TUNING

It is often found necessary, in order to expand the normal range of the guitar, to tune the sixth string ⑥ one tone lower to D (called **D tuning**) and, less commonly along with the fifth string ⑤ one tone lower to G (called **G tuning**).

Once either of these strings is tuned down it is, of course, necessary to play all fretted notes **two frets higher** than normal. This modification usually occurs, naturally enough, for pieces in the keys of D and D minor (D tuning) and G and G minor (G tuning).

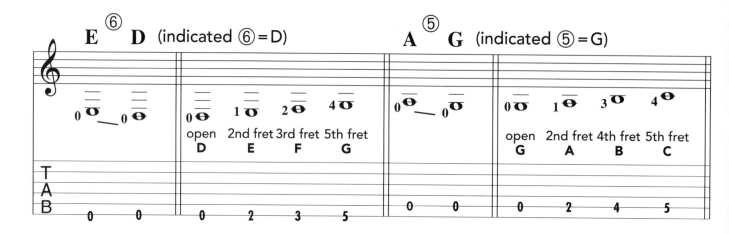

SCALES USING ALTERED TUNING

D MAJOR SCALE - (Shift from Ⅱ - Ⅶ Using First Unison F♯ ②)

⑥ = D

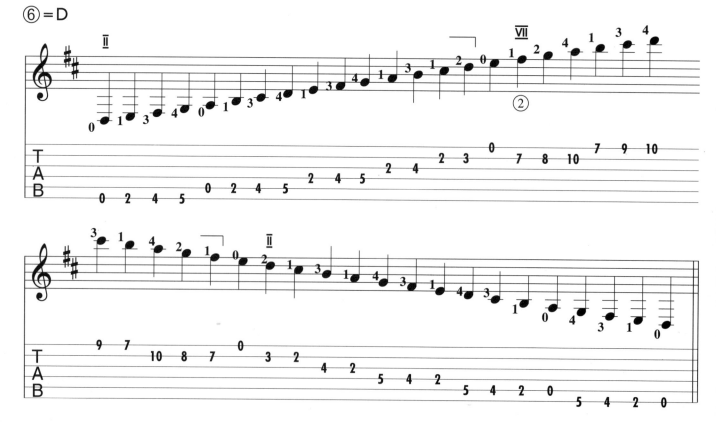

D MELODIC MINOR SCALE

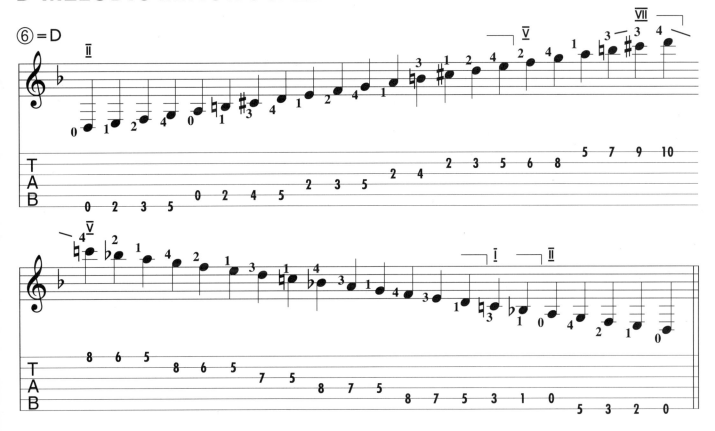

G MAJOR SCALE

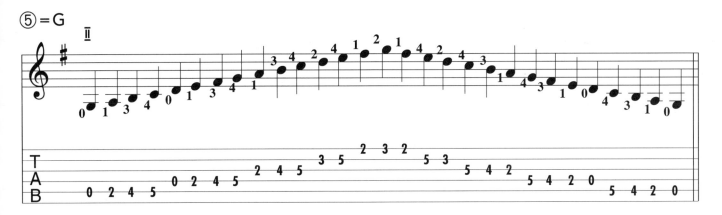

G MELODIC MINOR SCALE

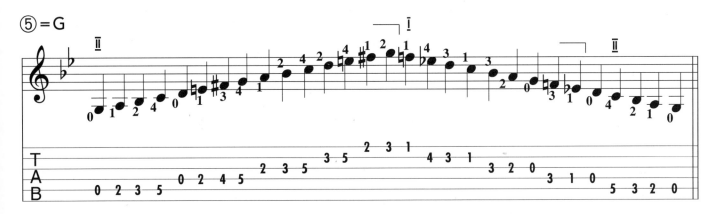

DEMONSTRATING ALTERED TUNING

D TUNING (Indicated ⑥ = D)

 23. Canon in D   Pachelbel

Note: Use of **inside half Bar** (tip segment covering ④ ③ and ②)
Also the use of a crotchet and minim together * for ease of notation and to indicate required note duration.

⑥ = **D**

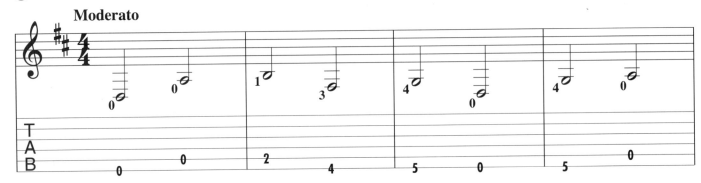

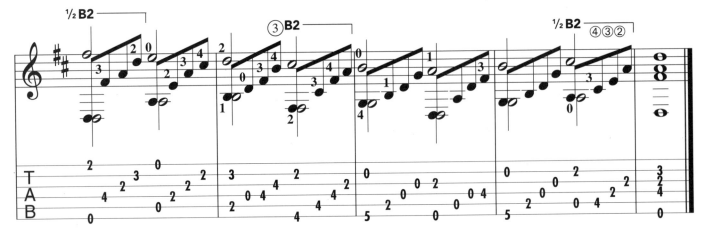

A full version of **Canon** by Pachelbel is available in **Popular Classics of the Great Composers Vol.2** and **Fingerpicking Classics Vol.2** along with many other pieces featuring altered tuning in both series of books.

G TUNING (Indicated ⑤ = G, ⑥ = D)

24. Wine, Women and Song

Strauss

⑤ = G   ⑥ = D

A full version of **Wine, Women and Song** is available in **Popular Classics of the Great Composers Vol.3.**

SYNCOPATION

Syncopation is the deliberate upsetting of the rhythm of a piece of music by displacing either the beat or accent. It occurs in music of all periods but has particular significance in jazz music and that of Afro American music.

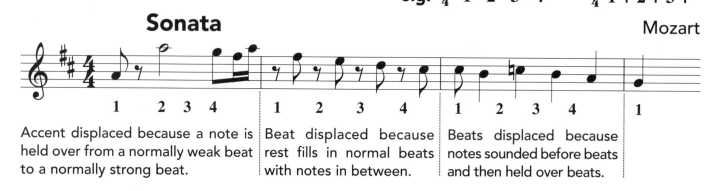

Sonata
Mozart

Accent displaced because a note is held over from a normally weak beat to a normally strong beat.

Beat displaced because rest fills in normal beats with notes in between.

Beats displaced because notes sounded before beats and then held over beats.

The Entertainer by Scott Joplin is one of the best and most famous examples of syncopation demonstrating a heavily syncopated treble line accompanied by a steady four beat bass line.

25. The Entertainer
Joplin

THE NINTH POSITION

NEW NOTES ON FRETS 11 AND 12

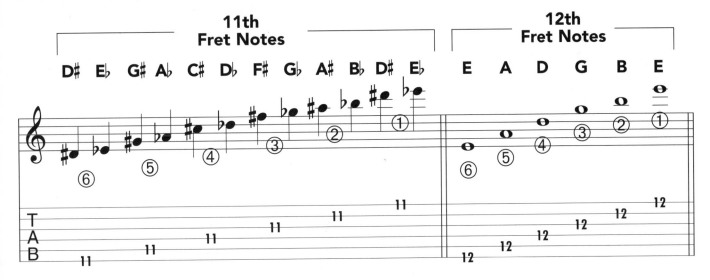

NINTH POSITION

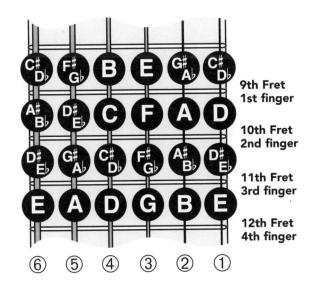

9th Fret 1st finger

10th Fret 2nd finger

11th Fret 3rd finger

12th Fret 4th finger

Note: Scales already studied in fifth position (page 123, C major and F major) and seventh position (page 135, D major and G major) can be duplicated in the ninth position as E major and A major, by using the same fingering two frets higher.

This means that every major scale can be duplicated this way by shifting up or down the fingerboard, i.e. fifth position, C major shifted up one fret, becomes C♯ or D♭ major (sixth position), seventh position D major shifted down one fret becomes D♭ or C♯ major, sixth position, etc.. This works by virtue of the fact that no open strings are used.

NINTH POSITION SCALES

E MAJOR SCALE - Using first position and ninth position (IX) shift to F♯ using 3 on ③ (second unison)

E MAJOR SCALE - Using primarily Ⅳ with shift to Ⅸ

E MELODIC MINOR SCALE - Ⅸ shift to F♯ using 3 on ③ (second unison)

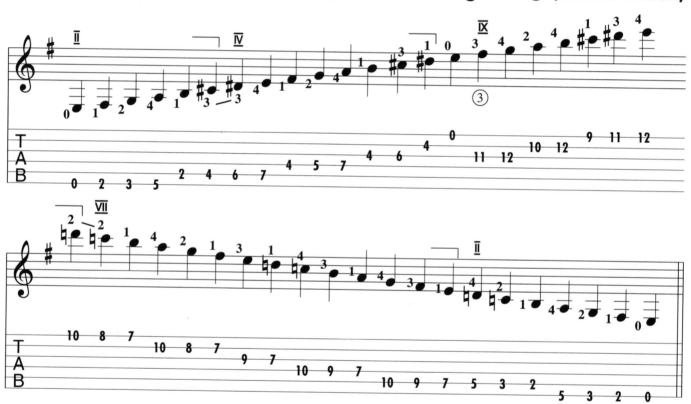

EXTENDED A MAJOR SCALE - Ⅸ shift to F♯ using 3 on ③

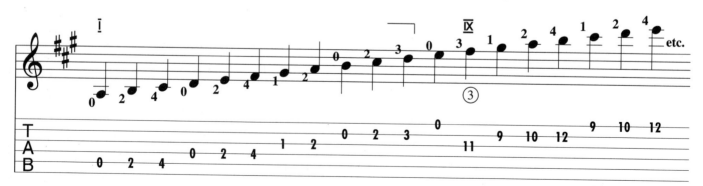

The following pieces, **Lesson in A**, **Duet in A** and **Fugue (duet)** demonstrate the **ninth position**.

Lesson in A uses the open E ① to move between IX and II as has been demonstrated in previous scale passages. **Duet in A** is more static and only leaves IX briefly in the second section. **The Fugue,** by nature of its single note structure, could be fingered in the lower positions but by way of demonstrating IX it has been fingered accordingly.

26. Lesson in A

Sor

27. Duet in A

Kuffner

28. Fugue (duet) - primarily in ninth position

Zipoli

Fugue (a latin word 'fuga' = flight) meaning that the voices or parts flee from one another.

Note: Introduction to $\frac{12}{8}$ time, where there are **twelve eighth notes per bar**.

158

Spanish Ballad, perhaps the most popular piece played on the classical guitar, is here presented in full. It is essentially an arpeggio piece with the melodic line as the top note of each group and as such the upper note (played by *a*) can be practiced as both a free and rest stroke. The E major section (key change to four sharps) has some difficult left hand stretches which must be practiced separately and includes a **double sharp(X)**, see page 146.

29 . **Spanish Ballad**

Anon

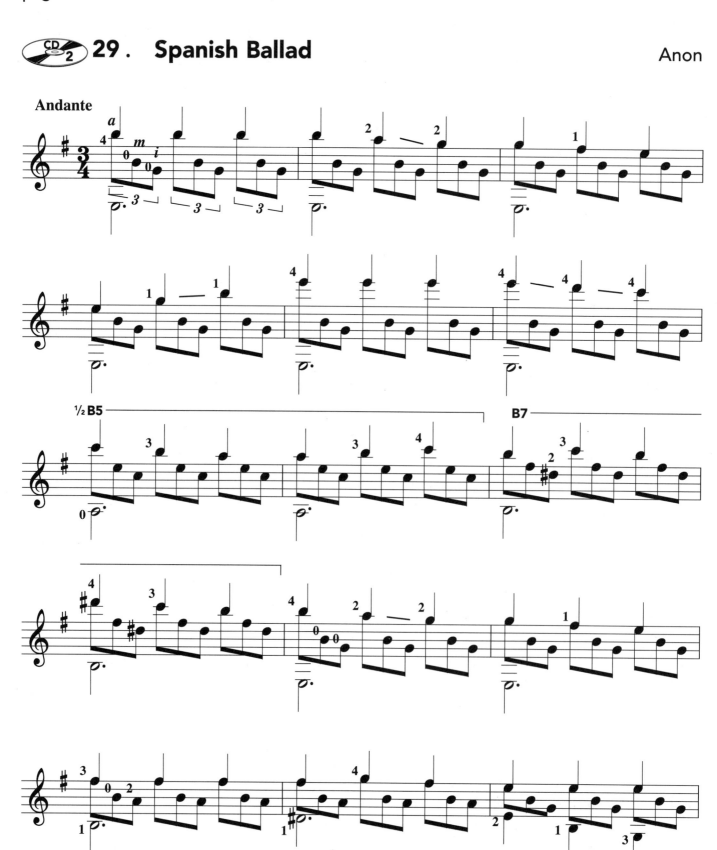

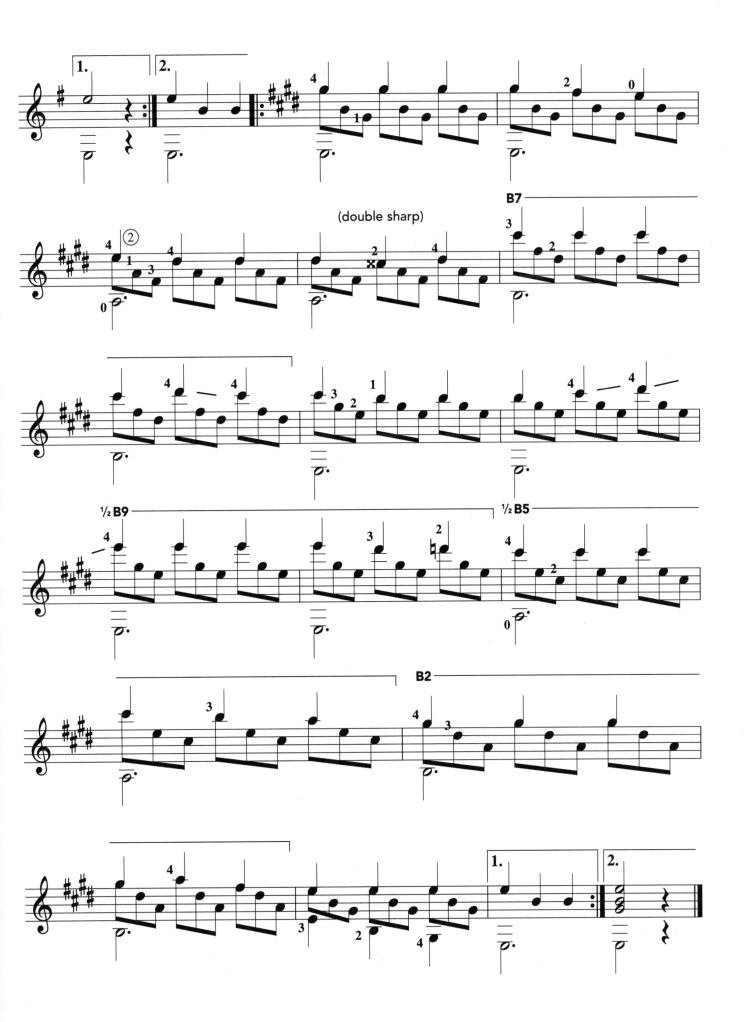

(double sharp)

VIBRATO

Vibrato is the effect produced to enhance the beauty of a note in singing or playing an instrument by subjecting the note to regular alterations of pitch varying from slow to very fast depending on the tempo or feel of the piece being played.

Vibrato can be achieved on the guitar by using either a sideways pushing and pulling of the string sometimes called **lateral vibrato** which is generally employed on frets 1-2 or the more important **length wise vibrato** (employed on fret 3 onwards). This method, which is related to (but not the same) as that used by violinists and cellists, is a beautiful effect which must nonetheless be used tastefully. As the name implies, the **length wise vibrato** is achieved by firmly pressing the desired note and, having plucked with the right hand, alternatively push the hand towards the nut then pull the hand towards the bridge until the note ceases to sound. This continuous pushing and pulling lengthwise has the effect of tightening and loosening the string and therefore raising and lowering the pitch, thereby helping to sustain and produce a singing quality to the note. Practice the vibrato chromatically i.e. 1, 2, 3, 4, 3, 2, 1, etc. firstly on the bass strings ④ ⑤ and ⑥ as a better grip can be obtained on the wound strings than on the clear nylon strings.

Ex. 1 begins with 1 on F♯ ④ (fourth position) working through chromatically 2 on G, 3 on G♯, 4 on A, counting the notes as indicated on each **push** and **pull** of the hand. This slow exaggerated movement sounds strange at first, but as the beats increase, (**Ex. 2** and **Ex. 3**), the sound becomes more like an acceptable vibrato. As shown below, practice this technique on all the strings in the fourth position before moving to other positions on the fretboard. Scales and melodies should also be counted this way until such time as the hand feels under control and ready to produce a less rigid, free vibrato.

CONTROLLED BEAT VIBRATO EXERCISE

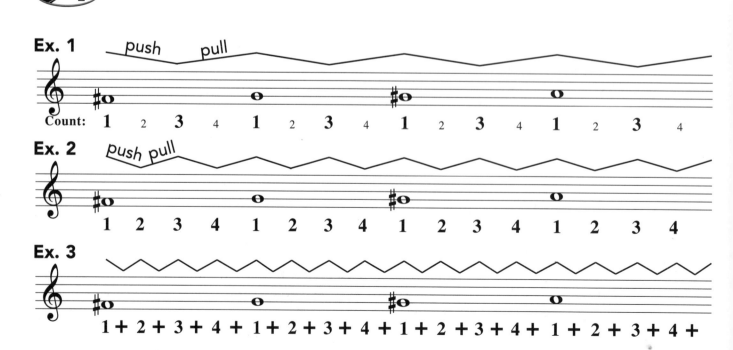

Try using a controlled beat vibrato on the melody line of the previous **Spanish Ballad**.

The following **Minuet in C** by Agustin Barrios is written in the style of the 19th century composers such as Sor, Giuliani, Aguado etc. and as such should be played graciously (Grazioso) and with a dance-like feel.

Being in the **Key of C** it often uses the third and eighth positions as indicated by the Bar signs. Note also the use of the **four string Bar** (✳) which uses the tip and middle segments of the first finger to cover ④, ③, ② and ①. Be sure to bend the middle joint to allow closer access for 2, 3 and 4 to the fretboard (see photo).

Four String Bar (⁴⁄₆ B)

31. Minuet in C

Barrios

Giuliani's **Norwegian Dance** demonstrates changes of key (modulations) from the opening E minor (key signature F#) to its relative major G major (key signature F#) back to E minor before changing to E major (key signature F#, C#, G# and D#) then returning D.C. al Fine through E minor. Whilst the same dance feel is retained throughout, the mood of the piece is changed dramatically by the constant changes of key, primarily dark and brooding in Em, a lighter, happy feel in G and an elated, sunny mood in E.

32. Norwegian Dance

Giuliani

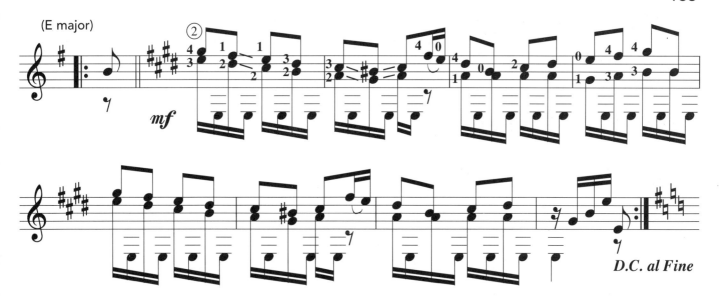

As its name implies **Lagrima** or **A Tear** is a slow, romantic piece which again uses a change of key (E major - E minor - E major) to convey strong mood changes. Use rest strokes on the single melody notes and be sure to differentiate between melody (upwards notes stems) and harmony (downwards note stems). Use **vibrato** where possible. Note the extensive use of **guide fingers** which can be practiced as **portamento** or **slide** (see page 138) depending upon taste and can be changed to either at anytime.

33. Lagrima (A Tear)

Tarrega

Carcassi's **Study in A** is generally regarded as one of the finest studies for the guitar because of its great technical and musical value. Use rest strokes as marked (∇) on the *a* finger notes and make the chord changes as smooth as possible.

34. Study in A

Carcassi

PRELIMINARY EXERCISES FOR STUDY IN A MINOR

Practice the following right hand exercises slowly and evenly. Only when the patterns are mastered will it be possible for **Study in A minor** (pg. 166) to flow freely and rhythmically. **Ex. A**, **B** and **C** occur in the first line and **Ex. D** is used as the last bar of each section. Take special note of the fingering: *p i m a m - i a m* (**Ex. D**), the gap between *m* and *i* being where the F to E snap occurs and that rest strokes (∇) are used on *m* to give an even, strong attack on the beat. Also take note of the shift to **second position** (3 on D♯) where special attention must be paid to the left hand thumb which moves with the first finger.

Another section which should be practiced separately is **Ex. E** which involves a shift to the **fourth position** (**G♯**). It is imperative to keep the left hand totally still as the fingers snap off the first string during this passage and use rest stokes as indicated.

35.

36. **Study in A minor**

Carcassi

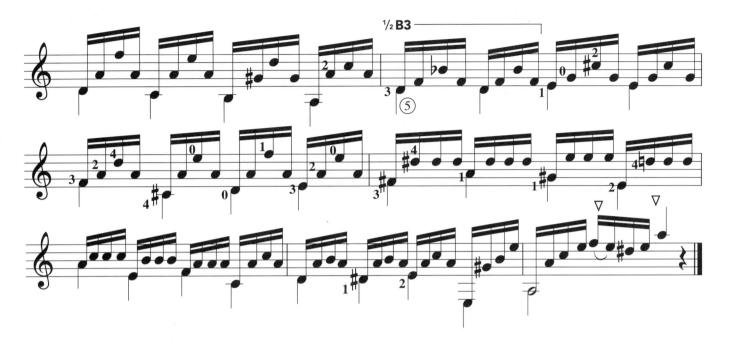

TREMOLO

The guitar is essentially a percussion instrument, meaning that once the note is struck the sound will inevitably begin to die. The most effective way to sustain a continuous sound is by a rapid succession of notes using alternating fingers on the one string called a **tremolo**.

There are many variations in the fingering of the tremolo however the model to be discussed here is the common classical guitar type as demonstrated in the preceding **Study in A minor** as **Ex. A** (*p a m i*). Because this example was used as a part of an arpeggio study it has a very strict four beat feel, whilst the ideal tremolo is more fluid and less percussive. Normally tremolo is notated as **thirty second notes** for the fingers and **eighth notes** for the thumb as seen below.

37.

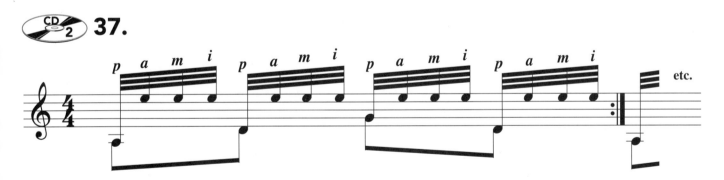

It can be observed that there is in fact a gap after each finger group whilst *p* plays a base or inner harmony. This gap is obvious at slow speed but at the required tempo the illusion of continuous melody notes is obtained. The tremolo should be practiced slowly as four even beats per group and, as with all exercises, it must be practiced strongly. The power and control attained this way will translate into fluency and smoothness at greater speed.

Be sure to retain a steady right hand position and an extended thumb (away from the fingers, see page 16, **photos A-E**). The tremolo will eventually be used on the inside strings ② and ③ (which of course presents the added difficulty of hitting adjacent strings) but for the moment concentrate on a strong, even sound on ①.

Try playing **Spanish Ballad** (page 158) and **Study in Em** (page 128) in tremolo as demonstrated below. Both pieces can be played this way, therefore they are ideal examples of **first string tremolo**.

38. Spanish Ballad (in tremolo)

39 (CD2) Study in Em (in tremolo)

Tarrega

LEGATO AND STACCATO

In general, music should be played in a **legato** or smooth, sustained manner, with very little interruption between notes. The opposite of **legato** is **staccato** (indicated by dots over the note, or rests after the notes to indicate the desired period of silence), which means to cut the note short to achieve a detached sound between each note. The period of silence between the notes is dictated by the rest following the note, or, in the case where a dot appears over the note, by the musical feel required by the player. The examples which follow give some idea of the degrees of staccato available.

Staccato is achieved almost entirely by the right hand fingers, although occasionally the left hand fingers can also be used by releasing the pressure on the string at the desired moment.

1. **Right hand thumb**
   After plucking E ⑥, immediately rest *p* back on the string (where the rest is indicated in the exercises below) which silences the note according to the rest as written, or musical taste (**Ex. 1**).
2. **Right hand fingers**
   Similarly, the right hand fingers should be replaced immediately after plucking both free and rest strokes, chords, etc..

In alternating staccato passages, the next finger to be used becomes the **staccato finger** (**Ex. 2**).

 **40.0**

Ex. 1

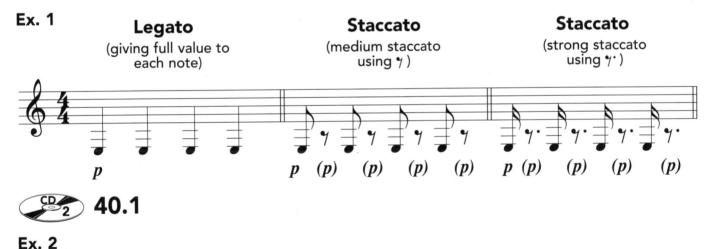

 **40.1**

Ex. 2

Right hand indication (i.e. (*p*), (*i*)) means to place on the string to both silence and prepare for the next note. Remember, a dot placed above the note ( ) indicates to use staccato as desired by the player.

Try playing familiar passages in staccato, i.e. **Right Hand Independence Exercises** (page 36), **Chopsticks** (page 41), **Slavonic Dance** (page 43), etc..

HARMONICS

Harmonics, the beautiful bell-like tones often heard in guitar music, can be produced by either of two methods.

1) NATURAL HARMONICS

Natural harmonics occur at nodal points along the length of each string, primarily at the 12th fret (half-length), 7th fret (one-third length) and 5th fret (one-quarter length). Another important harmonic point occurs at the 4th and 9th frets (as the same note), and this duplication happens for most harmonics on each string. These notes are demonstrated on the table below along with the seldom used 3rd fret harmonic. Harmonics are usually notated as a diamond-shaped note, and indicated as **Harm.** or **Arm.** , followed by a **Roman Numeral** for position or fret.

photo A: 12th fret Harm.

photo B: 5th fret Harm.

LOCATING NATURAL HARMONICS

To play a natural harmonic, in this case the first string, 12th fret E, lightly lay the fourth finger (straightened as shown in **photo A**) on the string, directly above the 12th fret. Pluck ① as normal, but immediately after plucking, lift the finger to allow the string to vibrate freely. Try the same above the first string, 5th fret (using the first finger as shown in **photo B**) and you will notice that it produces an E note two octaves higher than the open string (the 12th fret is the E note one octave higher than the open string). This is the same for all six strings.

It is advisable, when playing natural harmonics, to pluck close to the bridge (where no harmonic points occur) as opposed to over the sound hole (where several harmonic points occur) as it will nullify the desired harmonic if you pluck where a natural harmonic point is situated. Natural harmonics are most often written an octave below the actual pitch.

Table of Natural Harmonics

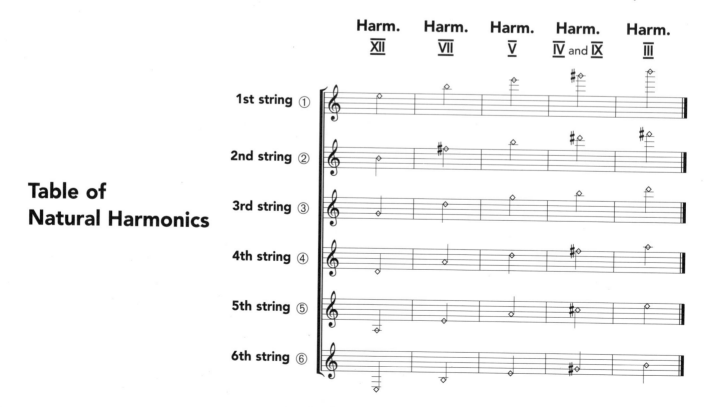

DEMONSTRATING NATURAL HARMONICS

41. Bells of Big Ben

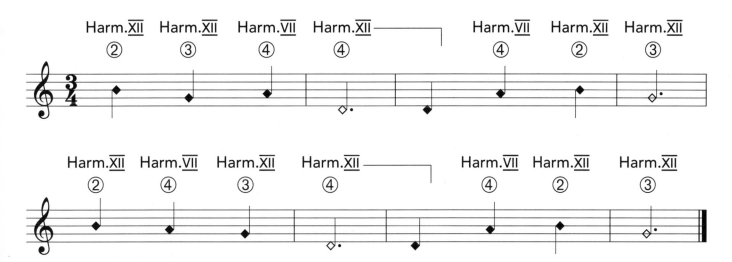

42. Ode to Joy

Beethoven

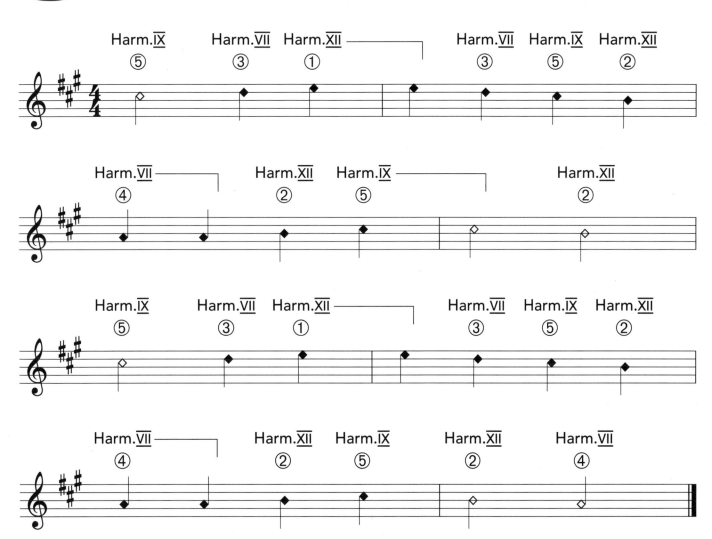

2) ARTIFICIAL (OR OCTAVE) HARMONICS *(written as: Harm.8va)*

Because **natural harmonics** only cover those harmonics found at natural nodal points on each string, it is necessary to use a different method to obtain all possible notes as harmonics. This is achieved by literally "halving" the string and producing the harmonics which would normally be found at the 12th fret and moving it chromatically or diatonically. As a left hand finger is employed to hold down the note (except in the case of an open string), it is necessary to use an entirely new right hand technique to both pluck the note and stop the string at the harmonic point which always occurs 12 frets above the stopped note. **Artificial harmonics** are written as normal notes on the stave, an octave lower than they sound. Therefore, if the F note at the first fret is required as a harmonic:

photo A

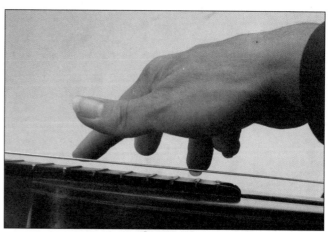

photo B

1. Locate F① as normal (1st finger)
2. Extend the *i* finger as shown in **photos A** and **B**, and move the right hand until the tip of *i* lays gently on the string directly above the 13th (F) fret.
3. Pluck the note with *a* and immediately remove *i* to allow the harmonic to sound.

This can be repeated on any note on all strings by moving the right hand to accommodate the extended *i* finger 12 frets above the fingered note.

Try playing first position scales on single strings (**Ex. 1**), then a scale moving across three strings (**Ex. 2**). Remember to adjust right hand (and arm) position when moving up or down the string.

 **43.**

Ex. 1
Harm.8va

Ex. 2

As this technique frees the right hand thumb, it is possible to play in conjunction with *p* bass notes (**Ex. 3**).

Ex. 3 Harm.8va

Play **Go Tell Aunt Rhody** (page 37) and **Old Kentucky Home** (page 38), using artificial harmonics on melody notes and *p* on the open **D** notes.

 44.   Go Tell Aunt Rhody

 45.   Old Kentucky Home

It is also possible to include another note with *m* to produce a three note chord with the harmonic note as melody (**Ex. 4** and **Study** by Carulli).

 46.

 47.   Study

Carulli

SECTION 5

NOTES ABOVE THE TWELFTH FRET

Notes on Frets 13 and 14

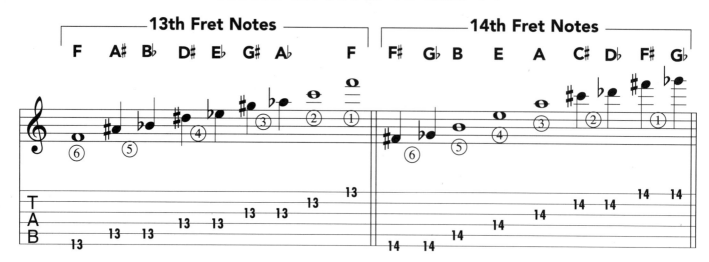

Notes on Frets 15 and 16

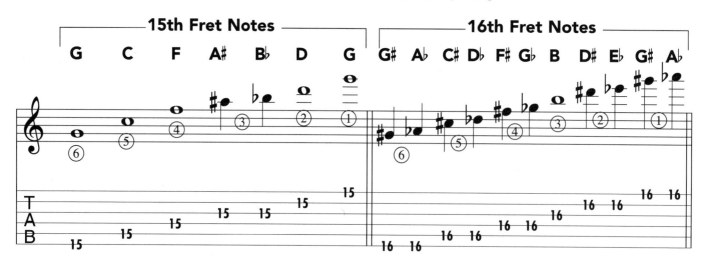

Notes on Frets 17, 18 and 19

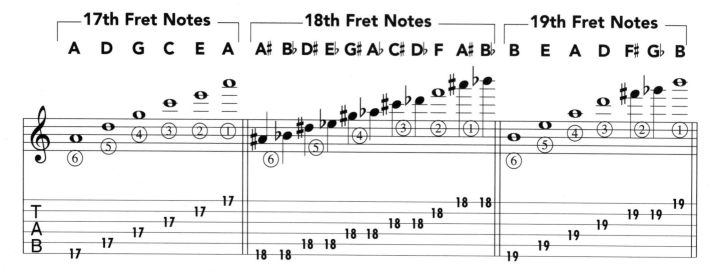

OPEN POSITION

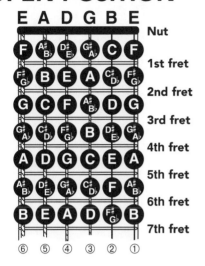

12TH POSITION

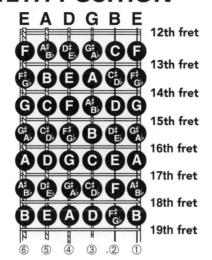

Note: the 12th fret is a repeat of the open position, one octave higher (see left).

PLAYING ABOVE THE 12TH FRET

photo A

photo B

photo C

As can be seen from the above photos, there is a significant change of left-hand position when playing above the 12th fret. **Photo A** shows the normal shape and angles of the first finger (as explained on page 31) as it plays at the ninth position (**C♯**) with chromatically positioned 2, 3 and 4 ready to play. **Photo C** shows the first finger having shifted to the seventeenth position (**A**). Notice how several changes have occurred:

1.   In **Photo C**, the elbow has moved away and the left wrist and forearm have dropped, along with the thumb, which still has contact with the **heel** of the guitar (see page 8).

2.   The shape of the first finger has changed to assume the **pyramid** shape of the half Bar (see page 81) whilst still pressing on its tip. This is the only first finger shape that allows close left-hand contact, thus allowing the remaining 2, 3 and 4 fingers to reach their required diatonic or chromatic notes. It is important to practice guiding the first finger alone from position 9 (**C♯** ① **Photo A**) to position 17 (**A** ① photo **C**) then return to position 9, gradually changing hand and finger position shape. **Photo B** shows the **interim** first finger shape at fret 13 as it guides from the normal shape (**photo A**) to that of **photo C**.

SCALES ABOVE THE TWELFTH FRET
CHROMATIC SCALE AT
IX (photo A)   XIII (photo B)   AND   XVII (photo C)

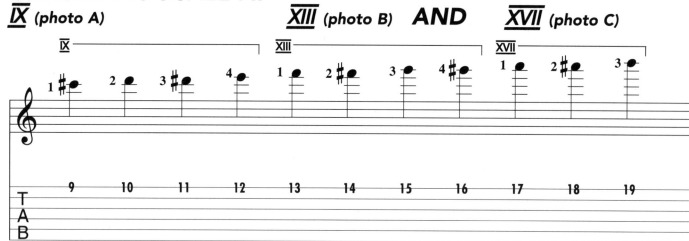

EXTENDED E MAJOR SCALE

THREE OCTAVE A MELODIC MINOR SCALE

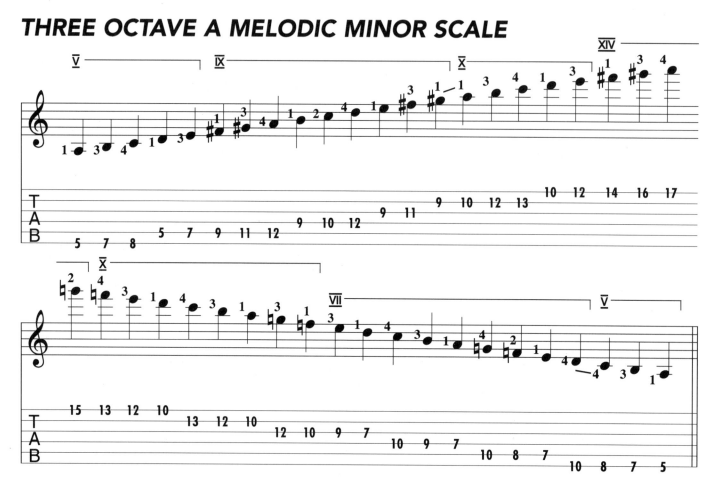

The following **Renaissance Dance** (Renaissance meaning the 14th - 16th century revival of arts and music) demonstrates playing above the 12th fret, in this case the 14th position, almost repeating that which has been played in the 2nd position. The repeated open bass notes (called **pedals**), along with the first finger guide from F#II - F#XIV facilitates this long distance shift. The piece also includes extensive ligados, as well as single and chordal natural harmonics.

48. Renaissance Dance

Anon

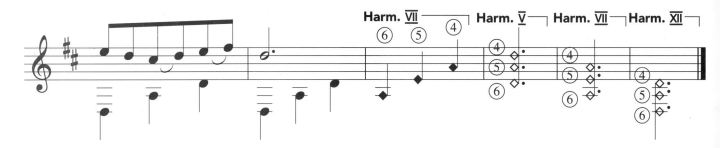

REST STROKE USING RIGHT HAND THUMB (*p*)

The student should by now be completely familiar with the use of free stroke *i*, *m*, *a* and *p*, along with rest stroke *i*, *m*, *a*. It is now time to explore the important technique of **rest stroke *p***. Rest stroke *p* is one of the most powerful techniques available to the guitarist as well as being one of the most difficult and misunderstood in terms of proper use. The rest stroke *p* is primarily used to produce a more powerful note than the free stroke, but it can also be used to stop a note sounding on an adjacent higher string, as will be seen in the following lesson on silencing basses (i.e. rest stroke on ⑥ automatically stops any note sounding on ⑤). The technique employed differs from free stroke *p*, in that *p* does **not** move independently of the hand (as demonstrated in "Thumb Plucking Action, Free Stroke" page 30), but rather retains a normal hand position with the thumb extended (see **photo A**). Proceed as follows:

photo A

photo B

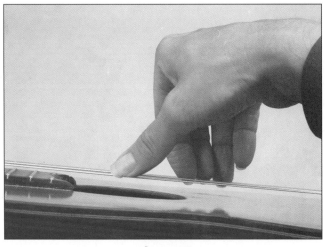

photo C

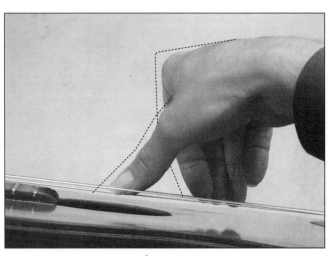

photo D

1.   Grip *i*, *m*, *a* on ③, ②, ① and execute a rest stroke *p* on ⑥ by moving the whole hand as a unit from the wrist (**photos A** and **C**) whilst allowing *i*, *m* and *a* to slide along the strings until the hand is prevented by the wrist joint from moving any further. This is shown by the dotted indication (**photos B** and **D**) and is usually about ½ inch (12mm) depending on each individual hand.

2.   Immediately after resting on ⑤, allow the right hand to relax back to the starting point (**photos A** and **C**) with *i*, *m* and *a* still lightly gripping ③ ② and ①. Do not allow the right hand to drop away and upset its normal perpendicular position during rest stroke *p* (**photos B** and **D**). Practice this technique using previous passages, i.e **Volga Boatmen** (page 42) **Slavonic Dance** (page 43) and the bass passages of **Hall of the Mountain King** (page 55).

REST STROKE *p* WITH CHORDS

Waltz (page 35) can demonstrate the use of rest stroke *p* on conjunction with *i*, *m*, *a* chords. Remember to allow the hand to relax back to its normal position after each rest stroke *p*, in order to play the *i*, *m*, *a* chords. Playing *p* rest stroke and *i*, *m*, *a* free stroke together (bar 4 and 8) requires a lot of practice and necessitates plucking the chords as the hand moves to accommodate the rest stroke *p*. Also practice the **Right Hand Independence Exercises** (page 36) using rest stroke *p*.

DOUBLE AND TRIPLE REST STROKE *p* (⅔)

It is possible, using the same technique as described above, to expand the rest stroke *p* to two and more strings. This enables a note on one bass string, i.e. ⑥, to be played almost simultaneously with another note, usually the melody, on the higher adjacent string (⑤). Try playing the following exercise, remembering to use the whole hand movement as practiced previously, on one string (⑥), then across two strings (⑥ and ⑤) and finally three strings (⑥, ⑤, ④). Obviously, it is not possible to sound both or all three strings together, but with practice the illusion can be achieved.

 **49.**

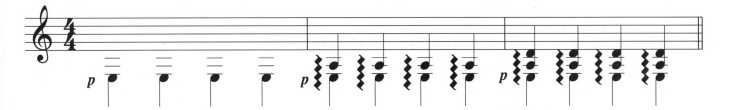

DEMONSTRATING SINGLE, DOUBLE AND TRIPLE REST STROKE *p*

 50. Waltz

Chopin

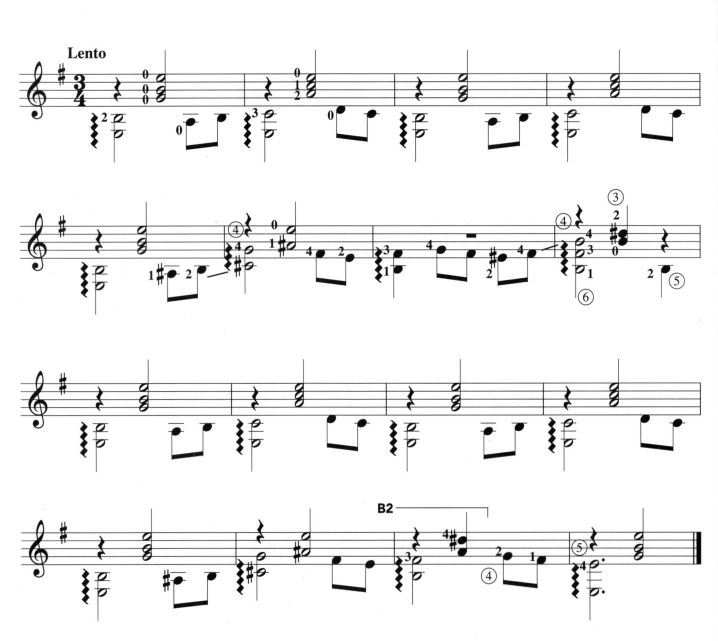

This double and triple rest stroke bass can and should be employed wherever possible, but it is especially worth mentioning the works of Heitor Villa-Lobos as being superb examples, i.e. **Prelude No.1, Prelude No. 2** and **Study No. 11**. Also, **Over the Waves** from *Popular Classics of the Great Composers Vol. 1* and **Melody in F** from *Popular Classics of the Great Composers Vol. 4*, clearly demonstrate the use of the double rest stroke *p*.

SILENCING BASS STRINGS

Because the guitar's bass strings (⑥ ⑤ and ④), once plucked, have a far greater sustain or time of sounding than that of the treble strings (③ ② and ①), it is important to control their duration (just as the dampening pedal on the piano), principally by using methods involving *p*.

METHODS OF SILENCING BASS STRINGS

1. **Pressure release of left hand finger** (indicated M.1)
2. **Rest stroke** *p* (M.2)
3. **Resting** *p* (M.3)
4. **Resting back of** *p* (M.4)
5. **Combining M.3 and M.4** (M.5)

1. **Pressure release of left hand finger:** This technique has already been used throughout the method (see section on staccato), and it is obvious that a fretted note, i.e. any note other than open string notes, will immediately cease to sound once the finger is removed from the string, thereby providing the desired silence (**Ex. 1**).

 51.

2. **Rest stroke** *p*: The preceding chapter (page 178) has already explained how a rest stroke *p* automatically silences the adjacent higher string upon which it rests (**Ex. 2**).

3. **Resting** *p*: Perhaps the most common method of silencing a bass string is to rest on the string using the pad of the thumb (*p*) as has been explained previously in the section on **staccato** (**Ex. 1**, page 169)

 **52.**

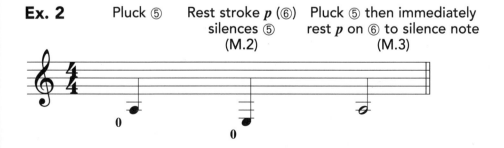

4. **Resting back of** p: Another method is to rest the small section of skin bordering the nail against a lower string immediately before (or after) plucking an adjacent higher string, i.e. pluck ⑥ and , just before plucking ⑤, push back against ⑥ with the back of p, before continuing on to pluck ⑤ as normal, rest or free stroke (**Ex. 3**, **photo A**).

 **53.**

Ex. 3   Pluck ⑥   Immediately prior to, or after plucking ⑤, rest back of p on ⑥ to silence note (M.4)

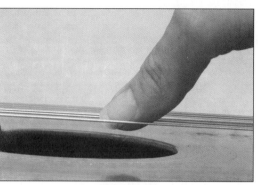

photo A

5. **Combining M.3 and M.4:** Two bass strings can be silenced together by inserting p between the strings, pressing against both simultaneously using methods **M.3** and **M.4** (**Ex. 4**, **photo B**).

 **54.**

Ex. 4   Pluck ⑥ and ⑤   Insert p between ⑥ and ⑤ silencing both simultaneously (M.5)

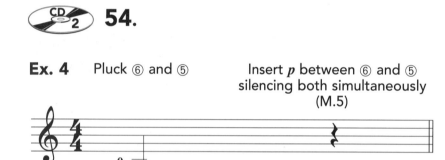

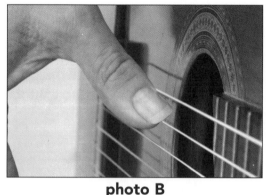

photo B

Try incorporating the different methods using previously studied pieces, i.e. **Study** (page 71), **Andante** (page 105), **Study in Ligados** (page 111), **Dance in A** (page 119), **Lesson in A** (page 155).

Remember that it is an extremely good idea to rest p on a bass string (using M.3) or strings (using M.5) when not in use, as it steadies the hand, prevents the guitar from producing unwanted overtones and harmonics (which may occur when playing certain notes on the treble strings) and provides a reference point for finding required bass strings. You will notice references for the different methods (M.2, M.4 etc.) in some of the pieces that follow.

USEFUL GUITARISTIC EFFECTS

PIZZICATO (Pizz.)

Pizzicato is an effect common to all stringed instruments, i.e. the violin, where the term means to pluck the string as opposed to the normal bowing. In guitar playing, pizzicato means to dampen the sound of a note or chord by:

1. Placing the palm of the right hand (nearest the little finger) in the groove behind the bridge saddle (see **photo A**).

photo A

2. Rolling the hand over to allow the fleshy side of p to strike ⑥, and at the same time allowing the palm to lay over the bridge saddle and lightly on the strings (see **photo B**).

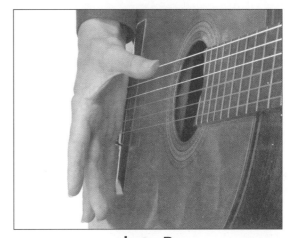

photo B

The combination of using the flesh of p to pluck the string and the muting caused by the palm resting on the strings, produces the pizzicato effect. Pizzicato is most commonly used in single note, scale-like passages and it is often necessary, when playing on the treble strings, to move the hand across to accommodate p (see **photo C**).

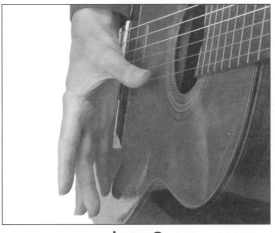

photo C

 **55.**

Pizz., hand position. as in **photo B**.

 **56.**

Pizz., hand position. as in **photo C**.

TAMBOUR (OR DRUM EFFECT)

Tambour is a seldom used percussive effect made by striking the strings just forward of the bridge saddle with the side of *p* and immediately raising the hand to allow the chord to sound.

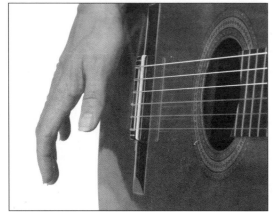

photo A: preparation

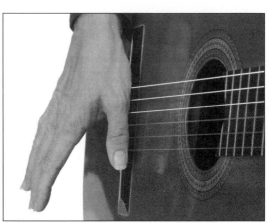

photo B: striking strings

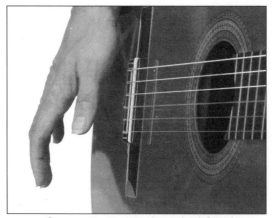

photo C: immediately lifted

 **57.**

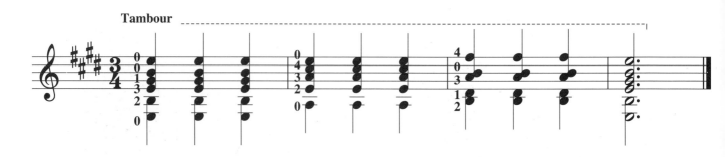

RASGUEADO

Rasgueado, the wonderfully varied strumming technique peculiar to Spanish flamenco music, is used sparingly in the classical guitar repertoire, mainly, of course, in Spanish pieces. Some of the most important rasgueado types are as follows:

Note: The direction of the strum, out or in, is indicated by the arrow.　　↑ **out**　↓ **in**

DUPLE STRUM

photo A: *i*, preparation

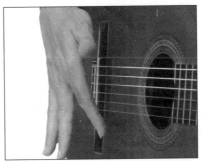

photo B: out strum completion

photo C: in strum completion

The following rasgueado examples are recorded at a slow tempo the first time through and at a faster tempo on the repeat to demonstrate both a practice and performance tempo.

 **58.**

This example uses **duples** (two beat) strums using one finger (*i* out and in), see **photos A - C** (above).

TRIPLET STRUM

photo A: *mi*, preparation

photo B: out strum (*mi* together), completion

photo C: in strum *m*, completion

photo D: in strum *i*, completion

 **59.** This example uses **triplets** (three beat) strums using two fingers (*i* and *m*), see **photos A - D** (previous page).

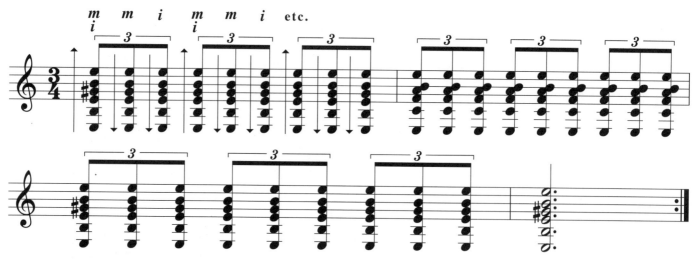

QUADRUPLE STRUM

photo A: *ami*, preparation

photo B: out strum (*ami* together), completion

photo C: in strum *a*, completion

photo D: in strum *m*, completion

photo E: in strum *i*, completion

 **60.** This example uses **quadruples** (four beat) strums using three fingers (*a*, *m* and *i*), see **photos A - E** (above).

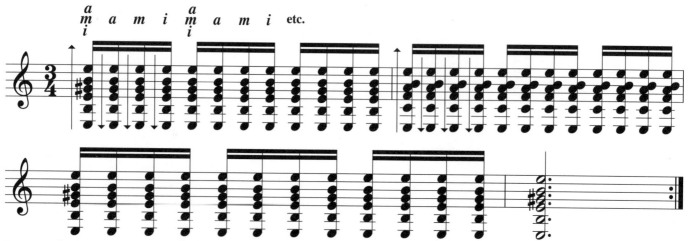

Remember to keep the right hand still during rasgueados and move only the fingers. Be sure to allow the tip joints of *a*, *m* and *i* to flex completely during **in** strums.

Notice also how each finger **remains straight** after the **out** strum in preparation for its **in** strum.

ARRANGING TREMOLO PIECES

The important elements to make a successful tremolo arrangement from an existing piece are as follows:

1. An elongated melody line without gaps
2. A base line which acts as the main beat supported by a moving harmony line
3. Relatively few string crossings for *a*, *m* and *i*

Some pieces work extremely well as tremolo adaptations, others reasonably well and others still are completely unsuccessful. Trial and error is the only way to judge this.

Note: Refer to page 168 for previous tremolo adaptions.

TREMOLO ON THE INSIDE STRINGS

The **tremolo** has previously been studied on the first string (①) and it is now time to expand its use to the ② and ③ as most tremolo pieces explore all three strings.
Because of the problem of adjacent strings when using tremolo on ② and ③, it is necessary to be a little more cautious with the finger action to avoid hitting other strings. There is no real trick to inside tremolo other than slow careful practice making sure to retain an even tempo and volume throughout.

I have adapted the following **Largo** (pg. 188) into tremolo using ① ② and ③ based on my arrangement in **Volume 3, Popular Classics of the Great Composers**, the opening bars of which are demonstrated below. If the student is familiar with the original arrangement, it will be obvious how the tremolo version works whilst making only minor alterations.

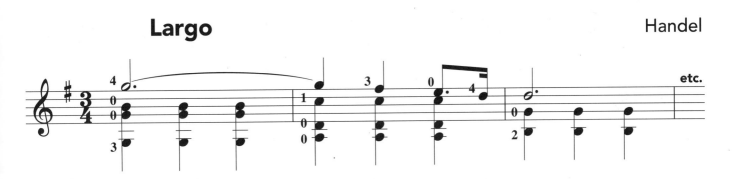

Largo — Handel

Following is a list of the most popular tremolo pieces readily available to the student once this magnificent technique is mastered:

*   **Recuerdos de la Alhambra, Sueno** (tremolo) by Francisco Tarrega
*   **Una Limosna por el Amor de Dios, Contemplation, Sueno en la Floresta** by Agustin Barrios
*   **Campanas del Alba** by Eduardo Sainz de la Maza
*   **Paisaje** by Emilio Pujol

61. Largo

Handel

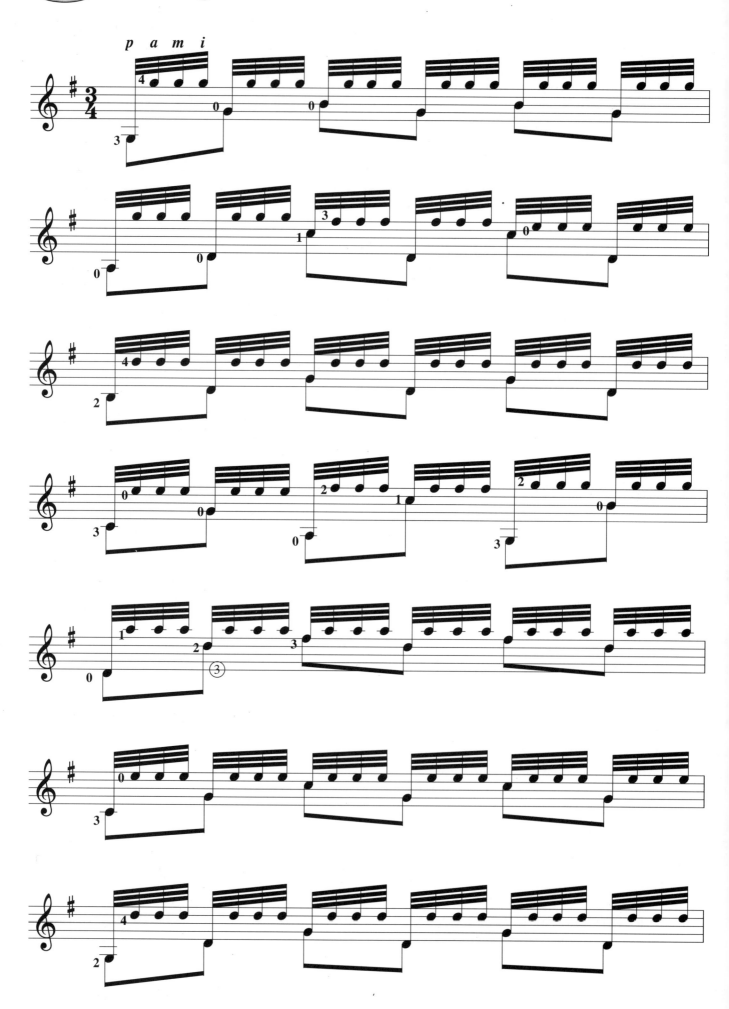

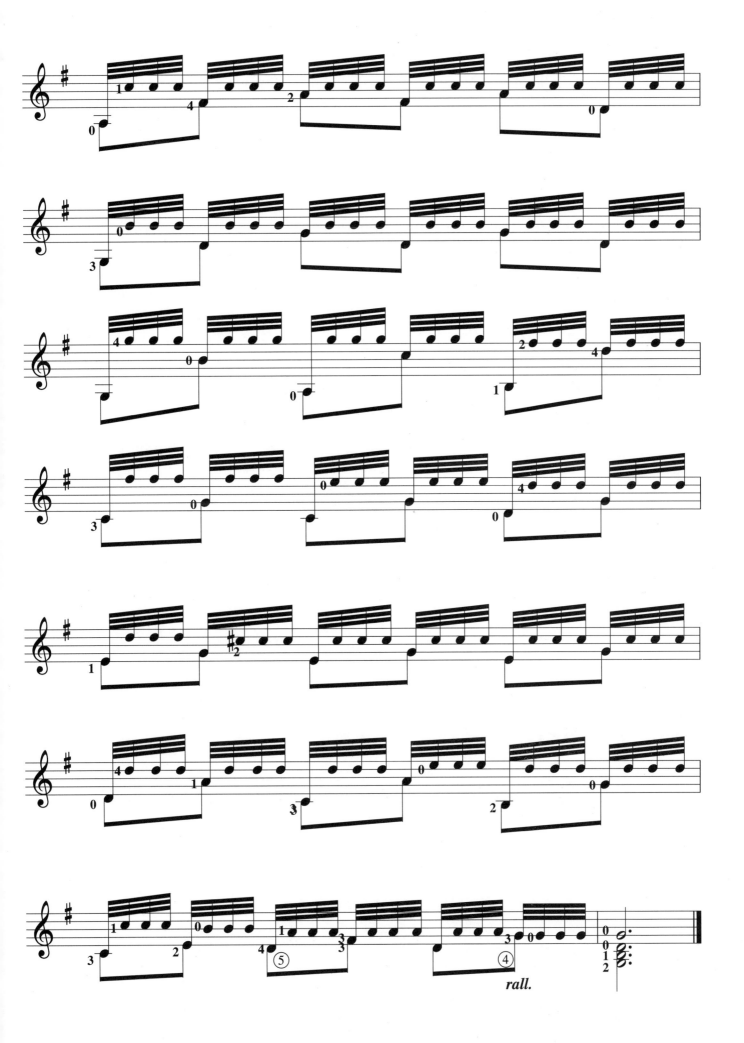

rall.

THE STUDY OF SCALES

Further to the study of scales, I would recommend the student acquire the Columbia Music Publications "Diatonic Major and Minor Scales" fingered by Segovia, as these are generally considered to be the standard, accepted fingerings. Various right hand plucking combinations are presented and should be practiced using both rest and free stroke.

COUNTING THE SCALE

Normally, scales are played as one note following another, with no real feeling of a time signature, however, the following **two octave C major scale** demonstrates, by means of counting, how a 4 or 3 beat feel can be obtained whilst playing the scale.

Use a combination of free and rest strokes: i.e., play a rest stroke on each counted note and free strokes on all other notes. Be sure to **count aloud** and continue playing until the first note, in this case, the C bass, is counted as 1. This requires 4 times through the scale for the 4 beat version, and 3 times through the scale for the 3 beat version.

 62. (Counting 3 beat version)

COUNTING THE TWO OCTAVE, C MAJOR SCALE

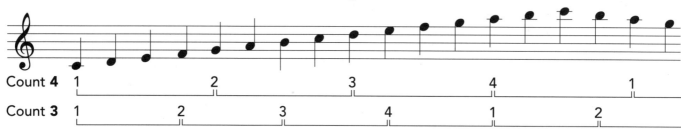

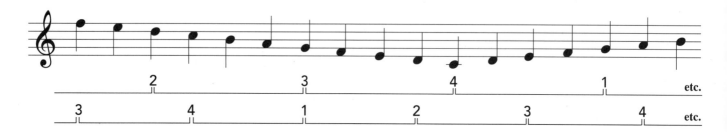

THE CHROMATIC SCALE

The chromatic scale (see page 50) is one of the most beneficial exercises for the development of the left hand fingers and positional movement of the left hand in general. For this reason, the following exercises are very useful. Remember to adjust hand position (as explained on page 31) when moving from ⑥ - ① or ① - ⑥.

Remember, the thumb must remain under **1** when moving up and down the fingerboard.

CHROMATIC SCALE EXERCISES

Ex. 1

Ex. 2   Repeat on all strings.

Ex. 3

The following four pieces present a variety of styles and periods and use many of the techniques described in this **Method**.

Estudio Poetico, written by one of Tarrega's most famous pupils, Daniel Fortea, should be played gracefully and freely. It has a very distinctive **common denominator** to be practiced separately, this being the right hand pattern, *a* finger (melody, usually rest stroke) followed by *i m* chord harmony. It also uses a type of **hinge** half Bar, which necessitates the first finger to drop onto the half Bar from a normal single note position, then return without the first finger leaving the fingerboard. Note also the use of **bass silencing methods** (M.2 and M.3). Use **rest stroke basses** wherever possible to provide depth to the harmony. Note also the **grace note** at the end of line 3 which is the same as that explained on page 118 except it is hammered instead of snapped.

63. Estudio Poetico

Fortea

This **Bourree**, (a baroque dance in 4/4 time) by the great J. S. Bach, is a very important and popular piece in the guitar repertoire. I have purposely left out any fingerings as it is intended to be used as both a solo and duet piece. Although written as a solo, the wonderful two-part writing works perfectly as a duet, and has been recorded as such to allow the student to play both the upper and lower parts separately with the recording. It can, of course, be refingered as a solo.

CD 2 **64. Bourree** (Solo or Duet)

J.S. Bach

The **Gigue,** (a lively baroque dance in $\frac{6}{8}$ time), should be played with a steady, uncompromising pulse at a reasonably fast tempo (allegro). It provides good practice in silencing basses, ligados, and alternating right hand fingering.

CD 2 **65. Gigue**

Weiss

* indicates where it is not vitally important to silence the bass note even though the timing suggests this.

Granadina uses many of the techniques studied throughout the method including tremolo, arpeggios, multiple slurs, half Bars and natural harmonics. It also contains an interesting syncopated section at line three, bar one. As with all pieces, practice each technique individually until it flows and can be incorporated into the piece as a whole.

66. Granadina (dance from Granada)

Trad.

For more books and recordings by Jason Waldron, visit his website at:
www.jasonwaldron-guitarist.com.au

MOVEABLE BAR CHORDS

As has been seen on page 144, "**Demonstrating the use of the Bar to play the same piece in a different key**", we can show the Bar's usefulness and versatility to find chords almost instantly by the use of **moveable Bar chords**.

ROOT SIX MAJOR BAR CHORD

We will begin by using the **Root Six Major Bar chord**, meaning two things. Firstly, the term **Root Six** indicates that the **Root** of the chord or the name of the chord is found on the **sixth string**. Secondly, the word **Major** points out exactly what type of chord it is.

The **Root Six Major Bar chord** is based upon the basic **E Major chord** and can be learnt in three steps.

Step One

Finger the basic E Major chord with the second, third and fourth fingers, therefore leaving the first finger free (we can think of it as being a "moveable nut").

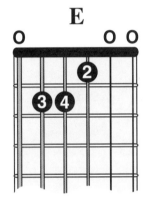

Note: O indicates open string

Step Two

Now move this fingering of the basic E Major chord up the fretboard one whole fret.

Step Three

Finally, **Bar** the first fret. By doing this your first finger is doing the same job as the nut except one fret higher. This completes the raising of the basic E Major chord by one fret. A new chord, F Major (see page 63), is produced because the F note (or F chord) is always found one fret higher than E. As mentioned above, the Root note (F) is found on the sixth string. The Root note will be highlighted by a box.

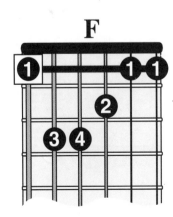

NOTES ON THE SIXTH STRING

The **Root Six Major Bar chord** can be played at any fret though the name of the chord will depend on which note the first finger is fretting on the sixth string. In order to determine exactly where a certain chord must be played it will be necessary to know the notes on the sixth string. The adjacent diagram illustrates the notes on the sixth string and gives three examples of the Root Six Major Bar chord.

In order to play a G Major Bar chord, position the Root Six Major Bar chord on the 3rd fret.

In order to play an A Major Bar chord, position the Root Six Major Bar chord on the 5th fret.

In order to play a C Major Bar chord, position the Root Six Major Bar chord on the 8th fret.

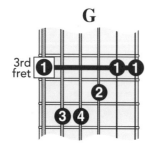

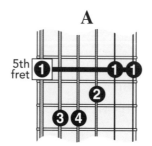

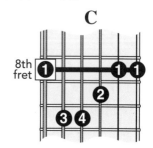

Other chord shapes using Root Six, Major, Minor, 7th chords etc. can be used the same way as follows.

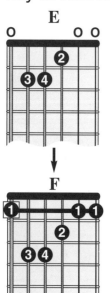

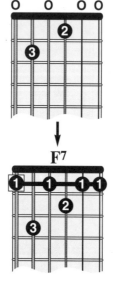

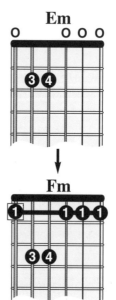

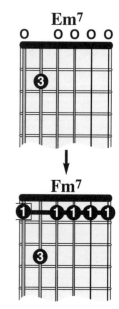

The following G chord shape uses the **third finger** as the **Root** of the chord.

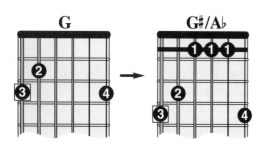

It may be found easier to use a **half Bar** on ②,③ and ④ on the G♯/A♭ chord.

ROOT FIVE MAJOR BAR CHORDS

As the term **Root Five** suggests, the **Root** (name) of these chords can be determined from the note on the **fifth string**, fretted with the first finger Bar. Like all Bar chords, the same shape can be moved up or down to any position on the fretboard. Adjacent diagram is the basic shape for the **Root Five Major bar chord**.

Note: X indicates the string is not played

NOTES ON THE FIFTH STRING

It will be necessary to know the notes on the fifth string in order to know on which fret a Root Five chord must be fretted. The adjacent diagram illustrates all notes on the fifth string up to the 13th fret. Try naming a chord and moving to the correct fret. Practice this until you can do it instantly.

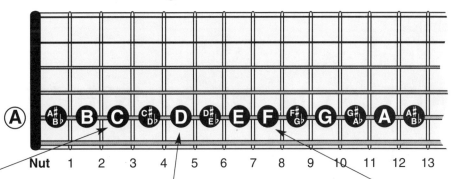

In order to play a C Major Bar chord, position the Root Five Major Bar chord on the 3rd fret.

In order to play a D Major Bar chord, position the Root Five Major Bar chord on the 5th fret.

In order to play an F Major Bar chord, position the Root Five Major Bar chord on the 8th fret.

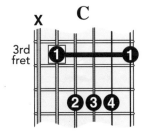
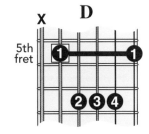
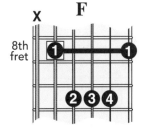

Other chord shapes using Root Five, Major, Minor, 7th chords etc. can be used the same way as follows.

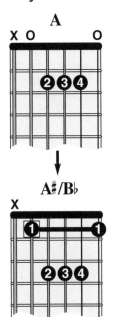
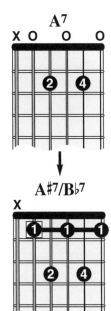
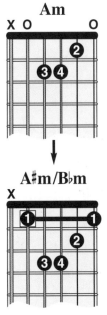
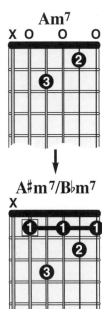

ROOT FOUR WITH OPTIONAL BAR

Bar chords are probably the most common example of moveable chord shapes. However, any chord which does not contain open strings can be moved to any position on the fretboard. Most moveable chord shapes follow the five basic forms found in open chords, i.e. C, A, G, E and D. Because Root Six Bar chords follow the basic shape of an open E chord, they can be described as E form chords. Root Five Bar chords follow the basic shape of an A chord, so they can be described as A form chords.

Root Four chords do not necessarily require a Bar, because the first finger can be used singularly on ④, thereby leaving 2,3 and 4 to finger the treble strings.

Root Four chords follow the basic shape of a D chord so they can be described as D form chords.

NOTES ON THE FOURTH STRING

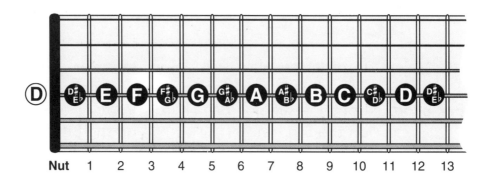

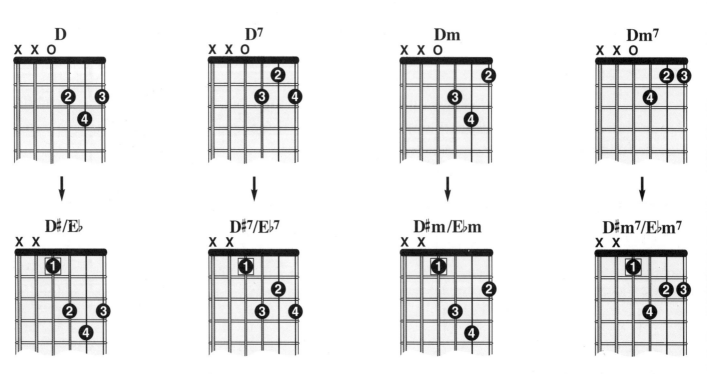

Notice that the position of the root note remains the same in each of these chords regardless of the chord type. This is the case with all bar chords as well as moveable chord shapes which do not require the use of a Bar.

MOVEABLE CHORD SHAPES IN FIVE FORMS

To develop a good understanding of the fretboard, it is important to have a system for identifying moveable chord shapes all over the fretboard in any key. Most moveable chord formations are closely related to the **five basic major chord shapes** shown below.

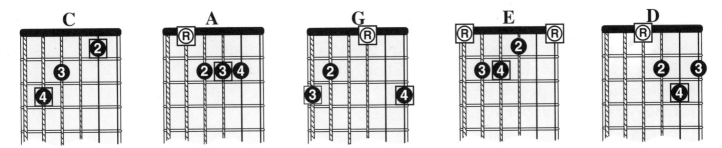

You already know the E form Bar chord (root 6) and the A form bar chord (root 5). The C, G and D chords can also be used as the basis for Bar chords. There are also many other moveable chord shapes based on these 5 shapes which are commonly used in music. The **five basic Bar chord forms** are shown below. Notice the order of these forms - **C, A, G, E** and **D**. This order is easy to memorize if you think of the word **caged**.

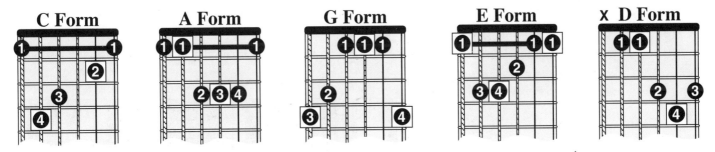

When these five forms (shapes) are placed end to end in the one key, they cover the whole fretboard. E.g. if you start with an **open C chord**, the **A form** Bar chord at the **3rd fret** is also a C chord. The **root note** on the **5th string** is shared by both chord forms. The A form chord then connects to a **G form** C chord beginning on the **5th fret**. The **root note** on the **3rd string** is shared by both chord forms. The G form then connects to an **E form** C chord at the **8th fret**. This time there are **two root notes** shared by both forms – one on the **6th string** and one on the **1st string**. The E form then connects to the **D form** at the **10th fret**, this time the shared **root note** is on the **4th string**. To complete the pattern, the D form connects back to the **C form** at the **12th fret**. The shared **root note** between these two forms is on the **2nd string**. This C form is **one octave higher** than the open C form. After this, the whole pattern repeats.

Practice the following using the five moveable shapes shown above. **Play each one as a C chord and name the new form out loud each time you change positions. It is essential to visualise the positions of the root notes in each form, as these remain the same for every chord type as demonstrated on the previous page. Once you can locate each form and it's root notes instantly**, repeat the exercise using a series of **G** chords, then **D** chords, etc. until you have covered every key.

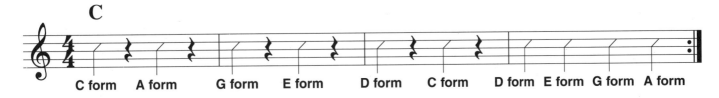

APPENDIX ONE – TUNING

It is essential for your guitar to be in tune, so that the notes you play will sound correct. The main problem with tuning for most students is that the ear is not able to determine slight differences in pitch. For this reason you should seek the aid of a teacher or an experienced guitarist.

Several methods can be used to tune the guitar. These include:
1. Tuning to another musical instrument (e.g. a piano, or another guitar).
2. Tuning to pitch pipes or a tuning fork.
3. Tuning with an electronic tuner.
4. Tuning the guitar to itself.

The most common and useful of these is the latter; tuning the guitar to itself. This method involves finding notes of the same pitch on different strings. The notation and diagram on the opposite page outline the notes used:

Tuning the guitar to itself requires a reference note from another source. Without this, your guitar may be in tune with itself, but higher or lower than the actual pitches on standard music notation. Start by tuning the open 6th string to either:

(a)   The open 6th string of another guitar.

(b)   A piano. You can also tune the other strings to the notes indicated on the keyboard below.

The piano note equivalent of the open 6th string is indicated on the diagram.

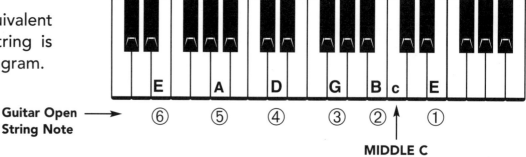

Guitar Open String Note → ⑥ ⑤ ④ ③ ② ①

MIDDLE C

(c) **Pitch pipes** which produce notes that correspond with each of the 6 open strings.

(d) **A tuning fork**. Most tuning forks give the note A.

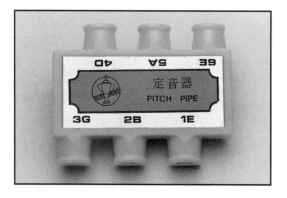

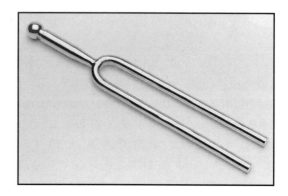

To produce sound from the tuning fork, hold it by the stem and tap one of the prongs against something hard. This will set up a vibration, which can be heard clearly when the bass of the stem is then placed on a solid surface, e.g. a guitar body.

TUNING THE GUITAR USING NOTATION AND TAB

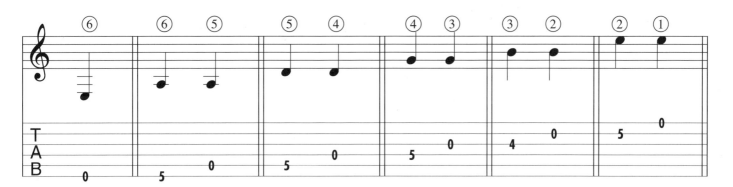

Unless you are using an electronic tuner, to be able to tune the guitar accurately usually requires many months of practice. You will probably need your music teacher or musician friend to help you tune when you are learning.

If you do not have another instrument to tune to, you can tune the guitar to itself by using the following method.

1. Place a left finger on the **6th** string (thickest string) at the **fifth** fret, and play the string.
2. Play the **open 5th string** (an **A** note). If this note sounds the same as the note you played on the **6th** string at the **fifth** fret, the **A** string is in tune.
3. If the open A string sounds **higher**, it means that it is **sharp**. Turn the tuning key slowly in a clockwise direction. This will lower the pitch of the string. Play the two strings again and compare the notes. Keep doing this until the open A string sounds the same as the E string at the fifth fret.

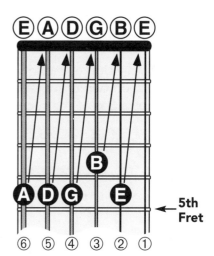

4. If the open A string sounds **lower**, it means that it is flat. Turn the tuning key slowly in a counter-clockwise direction. This will raise the pitch of the string. Play the two strings again and compare the notes. Keep doing this until the open A string sounds the same as the E string at the fifth fret.
5. Tune the **open 4th string** (a **D** note), to the note on the **fifth** fret of the **5th** string, using the method outlined above.
6. Tune all the other strings in the same way, except for the **open 2nd string** (a **B** note), which is tuned to the note produced on the **fourth** fret of the **3rd** string (see diagram).

ELECTRONIC TUNERS

Electronic Tuners make tuning your guitar very easy. They indicate the exact pitch of each string. It is still recommended however, that you practice tuning your guitar by the above method to help improve your musicianship.

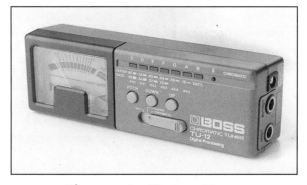

Electronic Guitar Tuner

APPENDIX TWO
GLOSSARY OF MUSICAL TERMS

'a' — annular finger (ring finger). As used for identifying the right hand fingers.

Accent — a sign, >, used to indicate a predominant beat.

Accidental — a sign used to show a temporary change in pitch of a note (i.e. sharp ♯, flat ♭, double sharp ✗, double flat ♭♭, or natural ♮). The sharps or flats in a key signature are not regarded as accidentals.

Ad lib — to be played at the performer's own discretion.

Allegretto — moderately fast.

Allegro — fast and lively.

Anacrusis — a note or notes occurring before the first bar of music (also called 'lead-in' notes).

Andante — an easy walking pace.

Arpeggio — the playing of a chord in single note fashion.

Bar — 1. A division of music occurring between two bar lines (also call a 'measure').
    2. When two or more strings are held down by one finger (usually the first finger) e.g. ½B2 indicates a Bar at the second fret covering three strings.

Bar line — a vertical line drawn across the staff which divides the music into equal sections called bars.

Bass — the lower regions of pitch in general. On guitar, the 4th, 5th and 6th strings.

Binary form — see form.

Chord — a combination of three or more different notes played together.

Chromatic scale — a scale ascending and descending in semitones: e.g. **C** chromatic scale:

ascending: C   C♯   D   D♯   E   F   F♯   G   G♯   A   A♯   B   C

descending: C   B   B♭   A   A♭   G   G♭   F   E   E♭   D   D♭   C

Clef — a sign placed at the beginning of each staff of music which fixes the location of a particular note on the staff, and hence the location of all other notes, e.g.

Coda — an ending section of music, signified by the sign ⊕.

Common time — an indication of 𝄴 time — four quarter note beats per bar (also indicated by **C**).

Compound time — occurs when the beat falls on a dotted note, which is thus divisible by three; e.g. ⁶⁄₈ ⁹⁄₈ ¹²⁄₈

D.C al fine — a repeat from the beginning to the word 'fine'.

Dot — a sign placed after a note indicating that its time value is extended by a half. e.g.

𝅗𝅥 = 2 counts   𝅗𝅥. = 3 counts

Double bar line — two vertical lines close together, indicating the end of a piece, or section thereof.

Double flat — a sign (♭♭) which lowers the pitch of a note by one tone.

Double sharp — a sign (✗) which raises the pitch of a note by one tone.

D.S. al fine — a repeat from the sign (indicated thus 𝄋) to the word 'fine'.

Duet — a piece of music written for two instruments.

Duration — the time value of each note.

Dynamics — the varying degrees of softness (indicated by the term 'piano') and loudness (indicated by the term 'forte') in music.

Eighth note — a note with the value of half a beat in ¼ time, indicated thus ♪ (also called a quaver).

Eighth note rest — indicating half a beat of silence, is written: ⅞

Enharmonic — describes the difference in notation, but not in pitch, of two notes; e.g.

F♯ or G♭

Fermata — a sign, ⌢ , used to indicate that a note or chord is held to the player's own discretion (also called a 'pause sign').

First and second endings — signs used where two different endings occur. On the first time through, ending one is played (indicated by the bracket ⌐1.   ⌐); then the progression is repeated and ending two is played (indicated ⌐2.   ).

Flat — a sign, (♭) used to lower the pitch of a note by one semitone.

Form — the plan or layout of a piece, in relation to the sections it contains; i.e. Binary form, containing an 'A' section and a 'B' section: (AB).

Forte — loud. Indicated by the sign 𝆑.

Free stroke — where the finger, after plucking the string, does not come to rest on any other string.

Half note — a note with the value of two beats in ¼ time, indicated thus: 𝅗𝅥 (also called a minim). The half note rest, indicating two beats of silence, is written: ▬◄— third staff line.

Harmonics — a chime like sound created by lightly touching a vibrating string at certain points along the fret board.

Harmony — the simultaneous sounding of two or more different notes.

'i' — index finger. As used for identifying the right hand fingers.

Improvise — to perform spontaneously; i.e. not from memory or from a written copy.

Interval — the distance between any two notes of different pitches.

Key — describes the notes used in a composition in regards to the major or minor scale from which they are taken; e.g. a piece 'in the key of C major' describes the melody, chords, etc., as predominantly consisting of the notes, **C, D, E, F, G, A,** and **B** — i.e. from the **C** scale.

Key signature — a sign, placed at the beginning of each staff of music, directly after the clef, to indicate the key of a piece. The sign consists of a certain number of sharps or flats, which represent those found in the scale of the piece's key. e.g.

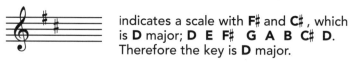 indicates a scale with **F♯** and **C♯** , which is **D** major; **D E F♯ G A B C♯ D**. Therefore the key is **D** major.

Lead-In — same as anacrusis (also called a pick-up).

Leger lines — small horizontal lines upon which notes are written when their pitch is either above or below the range of the staff, e.g.

Leger line

Legato — played smoothly, well connected.

Ligature — a line used to connect notes, e.g. eighth notes   ← Ligature

'm' — middle finger. As used for identifying the right hand fingers.

Major scale — a series of eight notes in alphabetical order based on the interval sequence tone - tone - semitone - tone - tone - tone - semitone, giving the familiar sound **do re mi fa so la ti do**.

Melody — a succession of notes of varying pitch and duration, and having a recognizable musical shape.

Metronome — a device which indicates the number of beats per minute, and which can be adjusted in accordance to the desired tempo. e.g. **MM** (Maelzel Metronome)   = 60 indicates 60 quarter note beats per minute.

Mode — a displaced scale e.g. playing through the C to C scale, but starting and finishing on the D note.

Moderato — at a moderate pace.

Modulation — to change the key within a piece.

Natural — a sign (♮) used to cancel out the effect of a sharp or flat. The word is also used to describe the notes **A**, **B**, **C**, **D**, **E**, **F** and **G**; e.g. 'the natural notes'.

Notation — the written representation of music, by means of symbols (music on a staff), letters (as in chord and note names) and diagrams (as in chord illustrations).

Note — a single sound with a given pitch and duration.

Octave — the distance between any given note with a set frequency, and another note with exactly double that frequency. Both notes will have the same letter name;

Open chord — a chord that contains at least one open string.

'p' — primary finger (thumb). As used for identifying the right hand fingers.

Passing note — connects two melody notes which are third or less apart. A passing note usually occurs on an unaccented beat of the bar.

Phrase — a small group of notes forming a recognizable unit within a melody.

Pitch — the sound produced by a note, determined by the frequency of the string vibrations. The pitch relates to a note being referred to as 'high' or 'low'.

Pivot finger — a finger which remains in position while the other fingers move.

Position — a term used to describe the location of the left hand on the fret board. The left hand position is determined by the fret location of the first finger, e.g. the 1st position refers to the 1st to 4th frets. The 3rd position refers to the 3rd to 6th frets and so on.

Quarter note — a note with the value of one beat in $\frac{4}{4}$ time, indicated thus ♩ (also called a crotchet). The quarter note rest, indicating one beat of silence, is written: ♩ .

Repeat sign — in music, used to indicate a repeat of a section of music, by means of two dots placed before a double bar line:

Rest — the notation of an absence of sound in music.

Rest stroke — where the finger, after plucking the string, comes to rest on the next string (for accenting the note).

Rhythm — the aspect of music concerned with tempo, duration and accents of notes. Tempo indicates the speed of a piece (fast or slow); duration indicates the time value of each note (quarter note, eighth note, sixteenth note, etc.); and accents indicate which beat is more predominant.

Rondo — A form of music based on the principle of a return to the initial theme.

Root note — the note after which a chord or scale is named (also called 'key note').

Semitone — the smallest interval used in conventional music. On guitar, it is a distance of one fret.

Sharp — a sign (♯) used to raise the pitch of a note by one semitone.

Simple time — occurs when the beat falls on an undotted note, which is thus divisible by two.

Sixteenth note — a note with the value of quarter a beat in $\frac{4}{4}$ time, indicated thus ♬ (also called a semiquaver).
The sixteenth note rest, indicating quarter of a beat of silence, is written: ♯

Slide — a technique which involves a finger moving along the string to its new note. The finger maintains pressure on the string, so that a continuous sound is produced.

Slur — sounding a note by using only the left hand fingers, indicated as ⌣ .

Staccato — to play short and detached. Indicated by a dot placed above the note:

Staff — five parallel lines together with four spaces, upon which music is written.

Syncopation — the placing of an accent on a normally unaccented beat. e.g.:

$$\frac{4}{4} \quad 1 \quad \overset{>}{2} \quad 3 \quad \overset{>}{4} \qquad \frac{3}{4} \quad 1 \quad \overset{>}{+} \quad 2 \quad \overset{>}{+} \quad 3 \quad \overset{>}{+}$$

Tablature — a system of writing music which represents the position of the player's fingers (not the pitch of the notes, but their position on the guitar). A chord diagram is a type of tablature. Notes can also be written using tablature thus:

Music Notation   **Tablature**

Each line represents a string, and each number represents a fret.

Tempo — the speed of a piece.

Ternary — A three part musical form.

Tie — a curved line joining two or more notes of the same pitch, where the second note is not played but its time value is added to that of the first note.

In Example 2, the first note is held for seven counts.

Timbre — a quality which distinguishes a note produced on one instrument from the same note produced on any other instrument (also called 'tone colour'). A given note on the guitar will sound different (and therefore distinguishable) from the same pitched note on piano, violin, flute etc. There is usually also a difference in timbre from one guitar to another.

Time signature — a sign at the beginning of a piece which indicates, by means of figures: i.e. $\frac{3}{4}$, the number of beats per bar (top figure), and the type of note receiving one beat (bottom figure).

Tone — a distance of two frets; i.e. the equivalent of two semitones.

Transcription — to arrange from one instrument to another, i.e. piano to guitar

Transposition — the process of changing music from one key to another.

Treble — the upper regions of pitch in general.

Treble clef — a sign placed at the beginning of the staff to fix the pitch of the notes placed on it. The treble clef (also called 'G clef') is placed on the second line indicated by the G note:

←— G line

Tremolo — a rapid repetition on one note.

Triplet — a group of three notes played in the same time as two notes of the same kind. e.g.:

Eighth note triplet

count: **1 + a**　　　**1 +**

Vibrato — a rapid vibration of a note (by the left hand fingers) to create slight pitch variations and a 'wavering' effect.

Whole note — a note with the value of four beats in $\frac{4}{4}$ time, indicated thus **o** (also called a 'semibreve'). The whole note rest, indicating four beats of silence is written: ■ ←— 4th staff line.